Passenger Liners of the World Since 1893

Revised Edition

Nicholas T. Cairis

BONANZA BOOKS • NEW YORK

NOTE TO THE 1979 EDITION: Much of the technical data has been revised, and additional information on last voyages and final dispositions of ships has been added.

Library of Congress Cataloging in Publication Data

Cairis, Nicholas T
    Passenger liners of the world since 1893.

    Published in 1972 under title: North Atlantic passenger liners since 1900.
    Includes bibliographical references and index.
    1. Ocean liners—Registers. 2. Ocean liners—History. I. Title.
HE566.025C35   1979   387.2'43   79-20985
ISBN 0-517-28875-3

CONTENTS

To Jehovah who has endowed me
with a love for the sea and ships
and to my mother and father.

The port of New York where all the great liners of the world have rendezvoused since the advent of the passenger ship to carry the many travellers to far off lands and resorts.

PREFACE

The term passenger liner is a label appropriate to steamships and motorships alike. The specifications governing a vessel of this type have undoubtedly fluctuated through the history of the passenger-carrying vessels. The phrase being entirely controversial, I have decided to include vessels only exceeding ten thousand gross tons and thereby keeping this volume within reasonable limits. In all there are enumerated two hundred and ten ships. Chartered ships and others completed to be released as war reparations or those which never sailed as passenger ships for the Lines respectively for numerous reasons . . . have not been included in this book. Concerning these ships there will be found in the fleet lists a brief note relating to their stories.

In the following pages I have gathered all such material pertaining to the most prominent steamship companies on the Atlantic Ferry today and those which have been there for some time. Some of the Lines have diverse services to other oceans, seas and continents of the world. My foremost interest was to include the better-known steamship company of each of the seafaring nations in the Western Hemisphere. In total there are thirteen of these Lines which fly the national flags of their homeland and the last of the Lines the Panamanian ensign owing to the once numerous interests in the company and also for keen tax purposes. I included this last Line as a type of international firm whose founders were of Greek, Swedish, Italian and American origin. The lore for the sea and ships has prompted me to choose not only the ships of my choice and liking, but to combine the greater number of all these liners in an unbiased factual publication of, hopefully, everybody's favourite ships. Each of the ships is illustrated with an original photograph to help the reader grasp the full beauty that emanates from all of these inspiring ladies from the great leviathans and express greyhounds to the intermediate and cargo-type passenger ships.

In stating the history of the ship's life, if there is any such to mention, there is listed in order if known: the builder and place of construction with the date; the last known tonnage; overall length and extreme breadth; moulded depth and number of propellers; type of propulsion and normal service speed; attained speed on trial runs or maximum speed; passenger accommodations (the given figures are usually the last in the ships' life and are in most cases smaller in the latter years of a ship than when she first entered into service because of the immigration laws of the early 'twenties and the reclassification of the classes brought about through the years); officers and crew (this in most cases follows the same rule as passenger accommodations because of the advancements of technology); maiden voyage; bulkheads and general number of decks (the labelling of decks is sometimes a controversial matter because of changes in construction and the naming by designers. Some may consider a certain section of a ship to be labelled a deck for passenger use whereas others may not, depending on the length or location of the section); history and ultimate fate; and last a sister ship or ships if any existed in the Line's services. Roman numerals preceding the name of a ship designate the numbered ship to carry the name.

This fast-moving era of air travel has almost outmoded the passenger ship into oblivion. Unable to maintain the tempo of the airlines of reducing once several-days' journeys to a mere couple of hours and the competition of rates the passenger ship has slowly, but reluctantly, moved out of the scene. Remorsefully, we are all witnessing the extinction of the passenger liner by the drastic drop in transatlantic sailings since World War II. Some of the larger fleets have depleted rapidly and many have employed their ships in cruising most of the year. Some have even gone to the point of selling cruise tickets to nowhere in which case the vessel merely sails around in circles just off the coast for a number of days. As time goes by the condition of the steamship companies seems to get dimmer in the possibility of a comeback to take her part in the travel medium which was rightfully hers. Though should the liner fade into the past, she will always live in the hearts of many who knew her in her day.

All facts have been entered in this book to the best of my knowledge. The information gathered stems from various sound resources as Lloyd's Register of Shipping, The American Record, newspaper articles, brochures, original abstract records and to some degree written and oral correspondence with the Lines and shipping personnel. Should the reader have any reason to argue its contents, which I believe to be the most accurate in existence, he may take the initiative to write me through the publishers and I would be most happy to try to assist him with the source of origination and degree of authenticity.

My gratitude would be incomplete if I should close without thanking the following people connected for supplying information and photographs for my book. They are enumerated thus: Mr Claros of the Spanish Line, Mr Vreugdenhil of the Holland-America Line, Mr Rickmann of the North German Lloyd, Mr Martin of the Cunard Line, Mr Bet of the Italian Line, Mr Bouvard of the French Line, Mr Martin of the United States Lines, Mr Henriksson of the Swedish-American Line, Mr Amundsen of the Norwegian-America Line, Mr Sigalas of the Greek Line, Mr Coutinho of the Portuguese Line, and Mr Tillet of the Home Lines. My thankfulness is also extended to Mr John L. Lochhead of the Mariner's Museum at Newport News, Virginia, Mark Sexton of the Peabody Museum in Salem, Massachusetts, Mrs Alice S. Wilson of the Steamship Historical Society of America on Staten Island, New York, The Upper Clyde Shipbuilders of Glasgow, Scotland, Mr David Pearson of Belmont, Massachusetts, and the Maritime Museum of Barcelona for photographs.

'If the only flags we gave allegiance to were the houseflags of the Lines and the only battles fought were for the Blue Riband.'

Nicholas T. Cairis

London, England

CUNARD LINE

I ALAUNIA

Builder: Scott's Shipbuilding & Engineering Co
Ltd, Greenock, Scotland.
Completed: November 1913.
Gross tonnage: 13405.
Dimensions: 538ft × 64ft. Depth 46ft.
Engines: Two four-cylinder quadruple expansion.
Screws: Twin.
Watertight bulkheads: Eight.
Decks: Four.
Normal speed: 14.50 knots.
Passenger accommodation: 520 cabin and
1540 third class.
Maiden voyage: Liverpool—Queenstown—
Portland, Maine—Boston on November 27,
1913.

Engaged in the London—Quebec—Montreal service in the summer months and to Halifax and
Boston during the winter with calls at Queenstown both east and westbound. On August 27,
1914 she sailed to Canada under war services and
did not return to London until February 14, 1915.
Resumed services from London to New York on
May 11, 1916 with calls at Falmouth and Plymouth eastbound. Sunk by a mine in the English

Channel on October 19, 1916 two miles from the
light-vessel, *Royal Sovereign*, after having disembarked her passengers at Falmouth, England
and with the loss of two lives. She and her sister
Andania were the first two ships built for the
Cunard Line's Canadian trade and the first to
inaugurate cabin-class accommodation over the
former labelled second class.
Sister ships: *Andania* and *Aurania*.

II ALAUNIA

Builder: John Brown & Co Ltd, Clydebank, Glasgow, Scotland.
Completed: July 1925.
Gross tonnage: 14030.
Dimensions: 538ft × 65ft. Depth 43ft.
Engines: Four steam turbines double-reduction geared.
Screws: Twin.
Watertight bulkheads: Eleven.
Decks: Four.
Normal speed: 15 knots.
Officers and crew: 270.
Passenger accommodation: 633 cabin, and 1040 third class.
Maiden voyage: Liverpool–Quebec–Montreal on July 24, 1925.

Employed in the Southampton–Quebec and Montreal services during the summer and to Halifax and Nova Scotia in the winter months. She calls at Cherbourg westbound and Plymouth and Le Havre eastbound. The *Alaunia* began her sailings from both Liverpool and London, but by 1928 was operating from Southampton. On August 24, 1939 she was requisitioned by the Admiralty for troop work and was fitted out at Gibraltar and sold to them on December 8, 1944 to be rebuilt as a base repair ship for engine room ratings at Devonport, England. Sold to the British Iron & Steel Corporation for scrap on January 5, 1957 and broken up at Blyth, Scotland on October 9, 1957.
Sister ships: *Ascania* and *Aurania.*

II ALBANIA

Builder: Scott's Shipbuilding & Engineering Co
   Ltd, Greenock, Scotland.
Completed: December 1920.
Gross tonnage: 12768.
Dimensions: 539ft × 64ft. Depth 47ft.
Engines: Four steam turbines double-reduction
   geared.
Screws: Twin.
Watertight bulkheads: Eight.
Decks: Two.
Normal speed: 15 knots.
Passenger accommodation: 80 cabin-class
   passengers.
Maiden voyage: Liverpool–New York on
   January 18, 1921.

Engaged in the Liverpool–New York run but on April 20, 1922, was transferred to the Liverpool–Quebec–Montreal run. She was built for maximum cargo capacity and limited accommodation for passengers. Staterooms were located on the shelter and 'tween decks. Unsatisfactory as a liner, she was laid up in 1925 and sold at the first opportunity. In 1930 the Italian firm of Liberia Triestina purchased the *Albania* and renamed her *California*. Sunk at an Italian port on August 11, 1941.

I ANDANIA

Builder: Scott's Shipbuilding & Engineering Co Ltd, Greenock, Scotland.
Completed: July 1913.
Gross tonnage: 13405.
Dimensions: 538ft × 64ft. Depth 46ft.
Engines: Two four-cylinder quadruple expansion.
Screws: Twin.
Watertight bulkheads: Eight.
Decks: Four.
Normal speed: 14.50 knots.
Passenger accommodation: 520 cabin and 1540 third class.
Maiden voyage: Liverpool–Quebec–Montreal on July 17, 1913.

Engaged in the London–Quebec–Montreal service in the summer months and to Halifax and Boston during the winter with calls at Queenstown, both east and westbound. *Andania* was the first of her type to enter service; built expressly for the Canadian trade and with her sister the *Alaunia* the first cabin-class liners. Requisitioned for work as a Canadian transport on October 14, 1914, until March 18, 1916. On May 2, 1916, she entered into the London–New York service with a call at Plymouth eastbound. On January 27, 1918, she was torpedoed and sunk by a submarine off Rathlin island, Northern Ireland, with the loss of seven lives.

Sister ships: *Alaunia* and *Aurania.*

II ANDANIA

Builder: R. W. Hawthorn, Leslie & Co Ltd,
  Newcastle-on-Tyne, England.
Completed: May 1922.
Gross tonnage: 13950.
Dimensions: 538ft × 65ft. Depth 43ft.
Engines: Four steam turbines double-reduction
  geared.
Screws: Twin.

Watertight bulkheads: Ten.
Decks: Four.
Normal speed: 15 knots.
Officers and crew: 270.
Passenger accommodation: 486 cabin and
  1187 third class.
Maiden voyage: London–Southampton–
  Quebec–Montreal on June 1, 1922.

Transferred to the Hamburg–Southampton–New York run from 1925 to 1926 when in 1927 she was diverted to the Liverpool–Quebec–Montreal run in the summer and to Halifax and Nova Scotia in the winter months calling at Greenock and Belfast eastbound and westbound throughout the year. World War II brought the need of merchant ships and the *Andania* like many others, was requisitioned and fitted out as an armed merchant cruiser in September 1939. She was torpedoed by submarine UA, 70 miles off Reykjavik, Iceland on June 15, 1940, and sank the next day.
Sister ships: *Antonia* and *Ausonia*.

ANTONIA

Builder: Vickers Ltd, Barrow-in-Furness, England.
Completed: December 1921.
Gross tonnage: 13867.
Dimensions: 538ft × 65ft. Depth 43 ft.
Engines: Four steam turbines double-reduction geared.
Screws: Twin.

Watertight bulkheads: Ten.
Decks: Four.
Normal speed: 15 knots.
Officers and crew: 270.
Passenger accommodation: 607 cabin and 1040 third class.
Maiden voyage: Liverpool–Quebec–Montreal on June 1, 1922.

Antonia made several voyages from Hamburg to New York, but in 1925 was scheduled permanently in the Liverpool–Greenock–Belfast–Quebec–Montreal service in the summer and to Halifax and Nova Scotia in the winter, also calling at Greenock and Belfast eastbound throughout the year. Converted to an armed merchant cruiser in October 1940 and sold to the Admiralty on March 24, 1942, for conversion to a repair ship and renamed *Wayland*. Sold for scrap in Scotland in 1948.
Sister ships: *Andania* and *Ausonia*

AQUITANIA

Builder: John Brown & Co Ltd, Clydebank, Glasgow, Scotland.
Completed: April 1914.
Gross tonnage: 45647.
Dimensions: 901ft × 97ft. Depth 55ft.
Engines: Four direct-action Parson steam turbines; three high pressure and one low pressure.
Screws: Quadruple.
Watertight bulkheads: Ten.
Decks: Six.
Normal speed: 24 knots.
Officers and crew: 550.
Passenger accommodation: 514 first, 410 second, and 865 third class.
Maiden voyage: Liverpool—New York on May 30, 1914.

The *Aquitania* had just completed three round trip voyages arriving at Liverpool on July 27, 1914, when World War I broke out in August and she was converted to an armed merchant cruiser, but incurred some minor damages whilst fitting out and was paid off by the Admiralty as being too large for operations. In the spring of 1915 she was used to transport troops to the Dardanelles, Turkey and then served as a hospital ship until 1917 in the Mediterranean. Laid up in 1917 and later transported American troops to France until March 1918. Resumed transatlantic services on June 14, 1919, from Southampton to New York and was refitted and converted to oil-firing between December 1919 and August 1920. Employed in the Southampton—Cherbourg—New York run and cruising on occasion. Requisitioned for troop service once again on November 21, 1939, this time extending until March 1948 when she was used for transporting American troops

after the war. Re-entered passenger service in May 1948 under arrangement with the Canadian Government whereby she made 12 trips to Halifax with her accommodation confined to a single austerity class. Commenced her last voyage for Cunard in November 1949 (Halifax—Southampton) arriving on December 1, 1949. During her career *Aquitania* steamed over 3000000 miles and carried approximately 1200000 passengers and crossed the Atlantic some 475 times. Her four propellers weighed $17\frac{1}{2}$ tons each and she was the first liner to have a gyro compass and to be equipped with Frahm's anti-rolling tanks. She was the last of the four-funnelled liners. Sold to the British Iron & Steel Corporation in February 1950 and left for the shipbreaker's yard at Garelock, Scotland, on December 19, 1949. A very majestic looking ship she had served the Line for 35 years and Britain throughout two world wars without a single incident of misfortune.

II ASCANIA

Builder: W. G. Whitworth & Co Ltd, Newcastle-on-Tyne, England.
Completed: May 1925.
Gross tonnage: 14440.
Dimensions: 538ft × 65ft. Depth 43ft.
Engines: Four steam turbines; two high-pressure double-reduction geared and two low pressure.
Screws: Twin.
Watertight bulkheads: Ten.
Decks: Four.
Normal speed: 15 knots.
Officers and crew: 367.
Passenger accommodation: 198 first and 498 tourist class.
Maiden voyage: London–Southampton–Quebec–Montreal on May 22, 1925.

Engaged in the Southampton–Cherbourg–Quebec–Montreal run in the summer and to Halifax and Nova Scotia in the winter calling at Plymouth and Le Havre eastbound and ending her voyages at London. On the night of December 14, 1934, the *Ascania* answered the distress calls of the sinking tramp steamer *Ulsworth* while in a mid-Atlantic gale. On July 2, 1938, she ran aground on Bic island, 150 miles off Quebec, but was refloated without difficulty. Requisitioned by the Admiralty for war services on August 24, 1939 and was fitted out as an armed merchant cruiser. She completed her duty work and arrived at Southampton on October 5, 1942, when she was reconditioned as a troopship and sailed as such on April 21, 1943, until the conclusion of the war. Resumed scheduled sailings from Liverpool to Halifax and Nova Scotia on December 20, 1947 and after being fully reconditioned in the autumn of 1949 re-entered services on April 21, 1950, from Liverpool to Quebec and Montreal. Reallocated to her home port of Southampton in March 1953 after an absence of 14 years and worked the Southampton–Le Havre–Quebec–Montreal route. She was the last of the Canadian fleet since the world war and made her last voyage for Cunard on October 26, 1956, from Southampton to Le Havre, Quebec and Montreal. Withdrawn from service in December and sold for scrap at Newport, Wales, leaving for the scrapyards on December 30, 1956.
Sister ships: *Alaunia* and *Aurania*.

III AURANIA

Builder: Swan, Hunter & Wigham Richardson, Ltd, Newcastle-on-Tyne, England.
Completed: September 1924.
Gross tonnage: 13984.
Dimensions: 538ft × 65ft. Depth 43ft.
Engines: Four steam turbines double-reduction geared.
Screws: Twin.
Watertight bulkheads: Ten.
Decks: Four.
Normal speed: 15 knots.
Officers and crew: 270.
Passenger accommodation: 633 cabin, and 1040 third class.
Maiden voyage: Liverpool–New York in September 1924.

Employed in the Southampton–Cherbourg–Quebec–Montreal run during the summer months and from Southampton to Cherbourg, Halifax and Nova Scotia in the winter months calling at Plymouth and Le Havre eastbound throughout the year and ending her trips at London. The *Aurania* had originally sailed from Liverpool and London, but by 1928 was operating from Southampton. On August 24, 1939, she was requisitioned for war service and was fitted out as an armed merchant cruiser. In July 1941 she collided with an iceberg while on convoy duty between Iceland and Halifax, but managed to escape serious damage until three months later when she was hit by a torpedo off the coast of Ireland but managed to make Rothesay Bay two days later. When first hit the *Aurania* listed 20 degrees to port and her number 3 hold was open to the sea with the adjacent number 2 hold flooding as well as the deep tanks, but the remaining watertight compartments kept her floating. Drydocking later revealed a hole 42ft × 38ft. Sold to the Admiralty on March 9, 1942, and converted to a fleet repair ship under the name of *Artifax*. Sold for scrap in Italy in January 1961.
Sister ships: *Alaunia* and *Ascania*.

II AUSONIA

Builder: W. G. Armstrong, Whitworth & Co Ltd,
  Newcastle-on-Tyne, England.
Completed: December 1921.
Gross tonnage: 13912.
Dimensions: 538ft × 65ft. Depth 43ft.
Engines: Four steam turbine double-reduction
  geared.
Screws: Twin.
Watertight bulkheads: Ten.
Decks: Four.
Normal speed: 15 knots.
Officers and crew: 270.
Passenger accommodation: 609 cabin, and
  1040 third class.
Maiden voyage: Liverpool–Cherbourg–Quebec
  –Montreal on June 22, 1922.

Employed in the London–Southampton–Quebec–
Montreal run from 1923 onwards during the
summer months and to Halifax and Nova Scotia in
the winter with a call at Cherbourg westbound and
at Plymouth and Le Havre homeward, ending her
trips at London. Fitted out as an armed merchant
cruiser on September 2, 1939, and sold to the
Admiralty on June 3, 1942. She was decommissioned in September 1964 and sold to Spanish
shipbreakers in August 1965.
Sister ships: *Andania* and *Antonia*.

BERENGARIA

Builder: Vulkan Werkes, Hamburg, Germany.
Completed: June 1912.
Gross tonnage: 52101.
Dimensions: 919ft × 98ft. Depth 63ft.
Engines: Four Curtis-A.E.G.-Vulkan steam
   turbines.
Screws: Quadruple.
Watertight bulkheads: Twelve.
Decks: Seven.
Normal speed: 23.50 knots.
Officers and crew: 950.
Passenger accommodation: 686 first,
   714 second and 1663 third class.
Maiden voyage: Southampton–New York on
   April 16, 1921.

Originally built for the Hamburg–American Line and christened *Imperator*. Ceded to Britain under the treaty of Versailles in 1920 and sold by the British Shipping Controller to a joint ownership between Cunard and White Star Lines and was renamed *Berengaria* in 1921.

Employed in the Southampton–Cherbourg–New York service year-round. She was converted to oil-firing between September 1921 and May 1922 and claimed a consumption of 750 tons per day. The *Berengaria* was one of Albert Ballin's great giants of whose running mates were the White Star Line's *Majestic* ex *Bismark* and the United State's Line's *Leviathan* ex *Vaterland*. During the depression years she acquired the nickname of 'Bargain Area' when rates were low and travellers few. Her aft funnel was a dummy. Caught fire at New York on March 3, 1938, and was subsequently

put up for sale after being labelled a fire risk by American authorities. Made her last voyage for the Line in March 1938 from New York to Cherbourg and Southampton and was sold to John Jarvis, shipbreakers at Jarrow, England, on November 7 of that year arriving in December. Work had been held up during the war and she was later towed to the Firth of Forth, Scotland, in 1946 and completely dismantled. As large and popular a steamer as the *Berengaria* was she never won the acclaim among the general public as did her consorts *Mauretania* and *Aquitania*.

Note: *Berengaria* made two voyages to New York prior to her renaming as such; on February 21, 1920, from Liverpool to New York and on June 16, 1920, from Southampton to Cherbourg and New York.

BRITANNIC

Builder: Harland & Wolff, Ltd, Belfast, Ireland.
Completed: June 1930.
Gross tonnage: 27778.
Dimensions: 712ft × 82ft. Depth 53ft.
Engines: Two ten-cylinder, four-stroke, double-acting Burmeister & Wain diesel.
Screws: Twin.
Watertight bulkheads: Twelve.
Decks: Five.
Normal speed: 18 knots.
Officers and crew: 485.
Passenger accommodation: 429 first, and 564 tourist class.
Maiden voyage: London–Le Havre–Southampton–New York in April 1935.

Built for the White Star Line. Passed to Cunard Line ownership on May 10, 1934 when the Cunard and White Star Lines consolidated. Engaged in the London–Southampton–New York service with a call at Le Havre homeward, and cruises. Requisitioned for troop work on August 29, 1939, and was attacked by Italian aircraft in the Red Sea in October 1940 and in January 1942 by U-boats and aircraft while on convoy, but managed to survive the war untouched. Decommissioned in March 1947 and resumed commercial sailings from Liverpool to Cobh and New York on May 22, 1948, after having been fully refitted. Each year the *Britannic* made a cruise to the Mediterranean which lasted some two months each trip. Her fore-funnel was a dummy enclosing the wireless room. The *Britannic* was the last ship to sail across the North Atlantic wearing the proud colours of the White Star Line. Commenced her last voyage on November 25, 1960, from New York to Liverpool, via Cobh. On December 16, 1960, she left Liverpool under her own power for the shipbreaker's yard at Inverkeithing, Scotland. Quite a dignified way to go to the scrapyard's that tear away the soul of a ship; it was the termination of the last vessel of one of the most famous steamship companies the world had ever known.

Sister ship: *Georgic*.

CAMPANIA

Builder: Fairfield Shipbuilding & Engineering Co Ltd, Glasgow, Scotland.
Completed: March 1893.
Gross tonnage: 12884.
Dimensions: 622ft × 65ft. Depth 45ft.
Engines: Two three-cylinder triple expansion.
Screws: Twin.
Watertight bulkheads: Twelve.
Decks: Three.
Normal speed: 21.50 knots. (She attained a speed of 23.02 knots during her trials.)
Officers and crew: 386.
Passenger accommodation: 526 first, 200 second and 300 third class.
Maiden voyage: Liverpool–New York on April 22, 1893.

Engaged in the Liverpool–Cobh–New York run. The *Campania* won the Blue Riband from the Inman Line's City of New York in May 1893 by making the run from Sandy Hook to Cobh in 5 days, 17 hours, and 27 minutes at a speed of 21.09 knots on her return maiden voyage. She was the first Cunarder to have twin-screws and had a promenade deck 370ft long. There were 12 main boilers and 96 furnaces which consumed over 20 tons of coal every hour to make her fast runs across the North Atlantic. In 1900 she rammed a sailing vessel in the St George's Channel sinking the ship and with the loss of all her crew. Still another mishap occurred in 1905 when an immense wave swept five persons overboard and injured several others. She made her 250th and last voyage in April 1914 and was withdrawn from service on

May 12, 1914, but made five Atlantic crossings under the management of the Anchor Line ending on October 15, 1914, at Liverpool. Sold to T. W. Ward in 1914 for scrapping, but reprieved from the shipbreaker's yard when she was resold to the Admiralty and converted to a seaplane carrier with considerable alterations forward and her forefunnel replaced by two others side by side. This now gave her three funnels which looked somewhat odd. Broke from her moorings on November 5, 1918, and foundered after colliding with the battleship *Revenge* in the Firth of Forth, Scotland. The half-submerged wreck was subsequently blown up, being a danger to navigation in the Firth of Forth.
Sister ship: *Lucania*.

II CARINTHIA

Builder: Vickers Ltd, Barrow-in-Furness, England.
Completed: August 1925.
Gross tonnage: 20277.
Dimensions: 624ft × 74ft. Depth 45ft.
Engines: Four steam turbines double-reduction geared.
Screws: Twin.
Collision bulkhead: One.
Watertight bulkheads: Nine.
Decks: Five.
Normal speed: 17 knots.
Officers and crew: 450.
Passenger accommodation: 240 first, 460 second, and 950 third class. (Accommodations are limited to 800 when in cruise service.)
Maiden voyage: Liverpool—New York on August 22, 1925.
Last voyage: New York—Liverpool on September 3, 1939.

Built as a dual-purpose ship she was employed in the Liverpool—Queenstown—New York run and cruising for which she is well remembered. Refitted in December 1932 and converted to a cabin- and tourist-class ship. The *Carinthia* left New York on January 7, 1933, for a world cruise that covered over 40000 miles and called at 40 ports. Transferred to the New York—West Indies cruise service in January 1936 after having been in the London—Channel ports—New York run two years prior. In 1937 one could cruise to Nassau and Havana out of New York in winter for as little as $85 for a nine-day holiday. The *Carinthia* made a world cruise every year between 1925 and 1933. Requisitioned as a liner-cruiser on September 2, 1939, and torpedoed by submarine U-46 off the Ulster coast of Ireland on June 6, 1940. After impact the *Carinthia* managed to stay afloat for 30 hours, but foundered on June 8. Two officers and two ratings were killed when the torpedo had hit. *Carinthia's* promenade deck was 390ft long and was as popular a ship as her sister, *Franconia*.
Sister ship: *Franconia*.

III CARINTHIA

Builder: John Brown & Co Ltd, Clydebank, Glasgow, Scotland.
Completed: June 1956.
Gross tonnage: 21947.
Dimensions: 608ft × 80ft. Depth 46ft.
Engines: Four steam turbines double-reduction geared.
Screws: Twin.
Collision bulkhead: One.
Watertight bulkheads: Nine.
Decks: Five.
Normal speed: 20 knots.
Officers and crew: 461.
Passenger accommodation: 174 first and 682 tourist class. (Accommodations are combined into one class when pleasure cruising.)
Maiden voyage: Liverpool–Greenock–Quebec–Montreal on June 27, 1956.
Last voyage: Montreal–Quebec–Greenock–Liverpool on November 25, 1966.

Engaged in the Liverpool–Cobh or Greenock–Halifax–New York run in the winter and sails from Liverpool to Greenock, Quebec and Montreal during the summer with some cruising. Equipped with motion stabilisers, and all public rooms are air-conditioned. She and her three sisters were all painted white in the winter of 1966–7 for cruise services. Sold to the Fairland Shipping Corporation in 1968 and renamed *Fairland.* Presently in their service under the Liberian flag.
Sister ships: *Carmania, Franconia* and *Sylvania.*

I CARMANIA

Builder: John Brown & Co Ltd, Clydebank, Glasgow, Scotland.

Completed: November 1905.

Gross tonnage: 19566.

Dimensions: 678ft × 72ft. Depth 52ft.

Engines: Three direct-action Parson steam turbines.

Screws: Triple.

Watertight bulkheads: Twelve.

Decks: Five.

Normal speed: 18.50 knots. (Attained a speed of 20.04 knots on her trials.)

Passenger accommodation: 425 cabin, 365 tourist, and 650 third class.

Maiden voyage: Liverpool–New York on December 2, 1905.

Employed in the Liverpool–Queenstown–New York run during the summer months and in the New York–Mediterranean services in the winter. Caught fire at Liverpool on June 4, 1912, but was not seriously damaged. On October 9, 1913, she rescued a number of persons from the Royal Line emigrant ship *Volturno* while ablaze in the Atlantic. Fitted out as an armed merchant cruiser on August 15, 1914, and engaged the Hamburg–South American liner-cruiser *Cap Trafalgar* off Trinidad on September 14, 1914. The *Carmania* performed heroically under the command of Captain J. C. Barr and sank the German liner sustaining 79 hits from the vanquished ship As the *Cap Trafalgar* sank fresh smoke appeared on the horizon and four funnels soon showed up. The *Carmania*, with her guns and the ship herself damaged, stoked her holds and steamed south-west by the sun and wind. It was later learned that the four-stacker approaching the scene had been the *Kronprinz Wilhelm,* the famous German raider coming to the

aid of her consort. *Carmania* is the only armed cruiser ever to have sunk a similarly outfitted merchant vessel as was the *Cap Trafalgar.* Decommissioned in 1916 she reverted to her owners and resumed sailings on November 9, 1916. Withdrawn from service from time to time during the war and laid up. Resumed scheduled sailings on December 21, 1918 from Liverpool to Queenstown and New York. Converted to oil-firing in 1923 and cabin-, tourist- and third-class accommodations. She opened a new service in the same year from Liverpool to Belfast, Quebec and Montreal. Reallocated to the Liverpool–Boston–New York run in 1925 and in 1926 she ran from London to Southampton and New York calling at Plymouth and Le Havre eastbound and from New York to Havana during the winter months. Made her last voyage for Cunard in August 1931 and was laid up at Tilbury dock until sold to shipbreakers in April 1932. *Carmania* was the first Cunarder to be driven by direct-action Parson steam turbines.

Sister ship: *Caronia.*

11 CARMANIA

Builder: John Brown & Co Ltd, Clydebank, Glasgow, Scotland.
Completed: August 1954.
Gross tonnage: 22952.
Dimensions: 608ft × 80ft. Depth 46ft.
Engines: Four steam turbines double-reduction geared.
Screws: Twin.
Collision bulkhead: One.
Watertight bulkheads: Nine.
Decks: Five.
Normal speed: 20 knots.
Officers and crew: 457.
Passenger accommodation: 117 first and 764 tourist class. (Accommodations are reduced to a single class when in cruise service.)
Maiden voyage: Liverpool—Quebec—Montreal on September 2, 1954.
Last voyage for Cunard Line: Southampton —Villefranche on August 1, 1971.

Employed in the Liverpool–Quebec–Montreal run she is the largest ship yet built for the Line's Canadian trade and is the first of four sisters. Reverted to the Southampton–Le Havre–Quebec–Montreal route on June 19, 1957, and was placed in the New York service in 1961 before undergoing an extensive refit at John Brown's as a dual purpose ship with renaming and cruised out of New York and Port Everglades in the winter. Reallocated to a fortnightly service from Port Everglades to the West Indies in 1968. The *Carmania* ran aground on January 14, 1969, on the island of San Salvador in the Bahamas while on a cruise with 471 persons on board. She was only damaged slightly with some leakage and was refloated on January 18 and repaired at Newport News, Virginia, USA. At the time of occurrence her passengers were picked up by a Coast Line steamer and disembarked where they could make arrangements for transportation. Refitted between March and November 1971 and placed in a permanent cruise service working out of Southampton to the Canary Islands, Iberian ports and the Mediterranean. Equipped with motion stabilisers and fully air-conditioned.
(See Notes on p. 223.)
Sister ships: *Carinthia, Franconia* and *Sylvania.*

1 CARONIA

Builder: John Brown & Co Ltd, Clydebank, Glasgow, Scotland.
Completed: February 1905.
Gross tonnage: 19782.
Dimensions: 678ft × 72ft. Depth 52ft.
Engines: Two four cylinder quadruple expansion engines.
Screws: Twin.
Watertight bulkheads: Twelve.
Decks: Five.
Normal speed: 18 knots. (Attained a speed of 19.62 knots on her trials.)
Passenger accommodation: 425 cabin, 365 tourist and 650 third class.
Maiden voyage: Liverpool–Queenstown–New York on February 25, 1905.

Employed in the Liverpool–Queenstown–New York service and New York–Mediterranean route in the winter months. Converted to a troopship in August 1914 and held until 1918 when she was released from government service. Resumed services on her regular route on January 11, 1919. Refitted and converted to oil fuel in 1920. Reverted to the Hamburg–Southampton–New York run in April 1922. In 1923 she was placed back in her original service and one year later was engaged in the Liverpool–Quebec–Montreal service. Reallocated once again to the Liverpool–Boston–New York run in 1925 and was finally settled in 1926 on the London–Southampton–New York run with a call at Plymouth and Le

Havre eastbound and winter employment cruising from New York to Havana. The *Carmania* and her sister *Caronia* were fitted with Stone-Lloyd hydraulic doors which could be operated from the bridge to shut the watertight compartments in case of emergency. Laid up in 1931 and sold to Hughes Bolchow, shipbreakers in 1932 for £20000 with delivery in July of that year. Resold to Japanese shipbreakers in 1932 for £39000 and sailed to Japan under the name of *Taiseiyo Maru*, which means, 'The Great Oceanship.' A well-earned calling for one of Cunard's loveliest ships. Scrapped by June 1933.
Sister ship: *Carmania*.

II CARONIA

Builder: John Brown & Co Ltd, Clydebank, Glasgow, Scotland.
Completed: December 1948.
Gross tonnage: 34172.
Dimensions: 715ft×91ft. Depth 53ft.
Engines: Six steam turbines; high-pressure, double-reduction geared; intermediate pressure and low pressure single-reduction geared.
Screws: Twin.
Collision bulkhead: One.
Watertight bulkheads: Nine.
Decks: Six.
Normal speed: 22 knots.
Officers and crew: 600.
Passenger accommodation: 581 first and 351 cabin class. (Accommodations are combined into a single class when pleasure cruising.)
Maiden voyage: Southampton—Cherbourg—New York on January 4, 1949.

Built as a dual-purpose ship but mostly for cruising. She is the largest single-funnelled liner in the world, and has a promenade deck 495ft long. The *Caronia* has six 45ft launches to carry her passengers ashore during cruises. The hull of the *Caronia* is painted in three shades of light green to blend with the *milieu* of her tropical cruises. On January 6, 1951, she left New York on a hundred-day cruise all over the world covering more than 8200 miles. Engaged in a cruise service to ports all over the world and works mostly out of New York with a few transatlantic voyages to Southampton via Le Havre each year. Commenced her last voyage for Cunard on November 18, 1967, and was subsequently sold to Universal Lines with renaming to *Columbia* in 1968; *Caribia* in late 1968. On March 11, 1969, an explosion occurred in the engine room and killed one man during a cruise off St Thomas. The ship was stalled and drifted for 20 hours before returning to St Thomas. She arrived at Curaçao two days later and was repaired at San Juan. Anchored in New York harbour in early 1970 and later moored at the United States Lines' dock at pier 86 in June 1970. Removed to pier 56 in June 1971.
(See Notes on p. 223.)

CARPATHIA

Builder: Swan Hunter Ltd, Newcastle-on-Tyne, England.
Completed: February 1903.
Gross tonnage: 13603.
Dimensions: 558ft × 64ft. Depth 41ft.
Engines: Two four-cylinder quadruple expansion.
Screws: Twin.
Watertight bulkheads: Eight.
Decks: Three.
Normal speed: 14 knots.
Passenger accommodation: 204 cabin and 1500 third class.
Maiden voyage: Liverpool–Queenstown–Boston on May 5, 1903.

Engaged in the Liverpool–Queenstown–New York run until March 5, 1904, when she entered into the Mediterranean trade from New York for a few voyages and also maintaining some voyages to New York from Liverpool. By September 1905 she was scheduled almost entirely in the New York – Funchal – Gibraltar – Naples – Palermo – Messina–Trieste–Fiume service with occasional calls at the Azores and Lisbon. Reallocated back to her original service from Liverpool to New York in July 1915. The *Carpathia* attained great fame for herself and her master, Captain Rostron when she answered the White Star Liner *Titanic's* distress calls on April 14, 1912, after she had collided with an iceberg at 11.40pm off the banks of New-

foundland on her maiden voyage from Southampton to New York. The *Titanic* had reported she was sinking by the head when the *Carpathia* sailing for the Mediterranean picked up the SOS and altered her course and ran for the scene where she arrived at about 4am on the following morning. *Carpathia* rescued the remaining 705 survivors of the 2208 on board that fateful night when the *Titanic* went down at 2.20am in latitude 41 46', longitude 50 14'. The *Carpathia* herself met with a similar fate when she was hit by three torpedoes 170 miles from Bishop Rock on July 17, 1918. Five men were lost when the torpedoes struck, trapping them in the boiler room.

CUNARD ADVENTURER

Builder: Rotterdamsche Droogdok Maats, Co
Rotterdam, Netherlands.
Completed: 1971.
Gross tonnage: 17500.
Dimensions: 484ft×72ft. Depth 41ft.
Engines: Four 12-cylinder Stork-Werkspoor
diesel engines.
Screws: Twin.
Decks: Five.
Normal speed: 20.50 knots.
Passenger accommodation: 740 first-class
passengers.
Maiden voyage: Southampton–Tangier–
Barcelona–Naples–Palma–Gibraltar–
Southampton on October 9, 1971.

She was purchased by the Cunard Line from Overseas National Airways while still on the stocks. Employed in a cruise service year-round from Southampton to Canary Islands and various Mediterranean ports that alternate almost each voyage. Fully air-conditioned and equipped with two Brown-AEG fins for stabilising the ship in rough weather. She is the first ship to carry a name alienated from the usual *ia* suffix with the exception of the Queens and the *Royal George*, which was a vessel purchased by the Line and not constructed for the Cunard Steamship Co as the *Adventurer* is. She is a product of the modern ship designer and most likely will cater to the modern traveller who more than likely will wear his formal dress the first night out. The *Adventurer* shows a vivid change in all that was once called the luxury liner. Presently in service.

DORIC

Builder: Harland & Wolff Ltd, Belfast, Ireland.
Completed: May 1923.
Gross tonnage: 16484.
Dimensions: 601ft × 68ft. Depth 41ft.
Engines: Four steam turbines single-reduction geared.
Screws: Twin.
Decks: Four.
Normal speed: 16 knots.
Passenger accommodation: 600 cabin, and 1700 third class.

Built for the White Star Line and passed under Cunard Line ownership when the two companies consolidated on May 10, 1934. Used solely for cruising while under Cunard-White Star ownership. She was damaged in a collision with the Compagnie des Transport's *Formigny* off Cape Finisterre, Portugal, on September 5, 1935, but was able to make the port of Vigo, Spain, for temporary repairs. Upon arrival at home it was decided that she be sold for scrap since no real use could be found for her. She was the only turbine-driven liner ever built for the White Star Line and was a very handsomely plain ship. Sold to John Cashmore, shipbreakers, at Newport, Wales, and left Tilbury dock, London, on October 7, 1935, for the yards.

I FRANCONIA

Builder: Swan, Hunter & Wigham Richardson Ltd, Newcastle-on-Tyne, England.
Completed: January 1911.
Gross tonnage: 18150.
Dimensions: 625ft × 71ft. Depth 40ft.
Engines: Two four-cylinder quadruple-expansion.
Screws: Twin.
Watertight bulkheads: Ten.
Decks: Four.
Normal speed: 16 knots.
Passenger accommodation: 300 first. 350 second, and 2200 third class.
Maiden voyage: Liverpool–New York on February 25, 1911.

Employed in the Liverpool–Queenstown–Boston run during the summer months and Liverpool–Queenstown–New York and New York–Mediterranean services in the winter. *Franconia* was the first Cunard liner to have a gymnasium installed.

Requisitioned for war service as a transport on February 15, 1915, and was sunk by a German submarine 200 miles north-east of Malta on October 4, 1916, with a loss of 12 lives.
Sister ship: *Laconia.*

II FRANCONIA

Builder: John Brown & Co Ltd, Clydebank,
 Glasgow, Scotland.
Completed: June 1923.
Gross tonnage: 20341.
Dimensions: 624ft × 74ft. Depth 45ft.
Engines: Six Brown & Curtis double-reduction
 geared turbine.
Screws: Twin.
Collision bulkhead: One.
Watertight bulkheads: Nine.
Decks: Five.
Normal speed: 16.50 knots.
Officers and crew: 434.
Passenger accommodation: 253 first, and
 600 tourist class.
Maiden voyage: Liverpool–New York on
 June 23, 1923.

Built as a dual-purpose ship. Engaged in the Liverpool–Queenstown–New York run, and cruising. In 1931 she was chartered to the Furness–Bermuda Line for five months of the summer season and for a shorter time the following year. Transferred to the London–Channel ports–New York run in 1934, but reverted back to her original run the following year. On December 24, 1938, she left Southampton on a world cruise that covered 41727 miles and called at 37 ports. Requisitioned for troop service on September 20, 1939, and carried over 149000 troops and steamed 320000 miles. In 1945 she was used as the headquarters at the Yalta conference in the Black Sea. During the course of her services as a transport she was damaged on her first trip out when the Royal Mail steamer *Alcantara* collided into her side on October 5, 1939, and smashed six of the *Franconia*'s lifeboats. Responsibility lay with the *Alcantara*'s poor method of zig-zagging while in the convoy. On June 16, 1940, the *Franconia* met with another close call when she was damaged by enemy bombers off the coast of Brittany, luckily none of the bombs made a direct hit but came so close they deranged her main auxiliary machinery. She then took on a heavy list and lost her lighting. Decommissioned in August 1948 after carrying displaced persons from Hamburg to Canada. The *Franconia* resumed sailings from Liverpool to Quebec on June, 1949. Ran aground on Orleans island just below Quebec in 1950 and remained there four days until she was refloated. Made her last voyage for the Line on November 16, 1956, from New York to Liverpool, via Cobh. *Franconia*'s promenade deck was 419ft long and was a most popular ship. Sold for scrap at Rosyth, Scotland where she arrived from Liverpool on December 18, 1956.
Sister ship: *Carinthia*.

III FRANCONIA

Builder: John Brown & Co Ltd, Clydebank, Glasgow, Scotland.
Completed: June 1955.
Gross tonnage: 22637.
Dimensions: 608ft × 80ft. Depth 46ft.
Engines: Four steam turbines double-reduction geared.
Screws: Twin.
Collision bulkhead: One.
Watertight bulkheads: Nine.
Decks: Five.
Normal speed: 20 knots.
Officers and crew: 456.
Passenger accommodation: 113 first and 731 tourist class. (Accommodations are combined into one class when in cruise service.)
Maiden voyage: Greenock—Quebec—Montreal on July 1, 1955.
Last voyage for Cunard Line: Port Everglades—Cobh—Cherbourg—Le Havre—Southampton—London on November 21, 1970.

Originally christened *Ivernia* and renamed *Franconia* in 1962. Employed in the Southampton—Le Havre—Quebec—Montreal trade with a call at Cobh eastbound. The *Franconia* made four round-trip voyages from London to Le Havre, Halifax and New York commencing on December 7, 1956, and was reallocated to the Southampton—Le Havre—Cobh—Quebec—Montreal run on April 17, 1957. Equipped with Denny-Brown motion stabilisers and fully air-conditioned. Reverted to the New York service in 1961 and overhauled at John Brown's in 1962 as a dual-purpose ship with renaming and cruising out of New York and Port Everglades in the winter. Reallocated to a weekly New York—Bermuda service in 1968 between March and November, and from December until March runs from Port Everglades to the West Indies. *(See Notes on p. 223.)*
Sister ships: *Carinthia, Carmania,* and *Sylvania.*

GEORGIC

Builder: Harland & Wolff Ltd, Belfast, Ireland.
Completed: June 1932.
Gross tonnage: 27469.
Dimensions: 712ft × 82ft. Depth 53ft.
Engines: Two Burmeister & Wain ten-cylinder, four-stroke, double-acting diesel.
Screws: Twin.
Watertight bulkheads: Twelve.
Decks: Five.
Normal speed: 18 knots.
Officers and crew: 485.
Passenger accommodation: 429 first and 564 tourist class.
Maiden voyage: London–New York in April 1935.

Built for the White Star Line. Passed on to Cunard ownership on May 10, 1934 when the two companies consolidated. Engaged in the London–Channel ports–New York service which cruises from New York to the West Indies during the winter months. Requisitioned for troop work on March 1940 and was gutted by fire off Tewfik in the Suez Canal when fired upon by enemy aircraft at 2am on July 14, 1941. She ran aground with her engine room flooded 18ft high. Refloated on October 27 and sailed from the Suez under tow on December 28 arriving at Port Sudan on January 10, 1942, where she was repaired temporarily. Towed to Karachi, Pakistan, on March 31 for further work and sailed under her own power at a speed of 10–11 knots on December 11 for Bombay where she arrived two days later. Repaired and sailed on January 20, 1943, at a speed of 16 knots for Liverpool. She was taken to Harland & Wolff and rebuilt as a permanent transport with one mast and a funnel gone. She was then sold to the Ministry of Transport and was after December 1944 chartered by the Cunard Line. Chartered by Cunard for six round trips from Liverpool to Cobh and New York on May 4, 1950, and for seven or so similar trips each year until her last voyage from New York to Halifax, Cobh, Le Havre and Southampton on October 19, 1954. Chartered by the Australian Government in May 1955 and sold for scrap in January 1956 where she arrived at Faslane, Garelock, Scotland on February 1, 1956.
Sister ship: *Britannic.*

HOMERIC

Builder: F. Schichau, Danzig, Germany.
Completed: 1920.
Gross tonnage: 34351.
Dimensions: 776ft × 83ft. Depth 49ft.
Engines: Two four-cylinder triple expansion.
Screws: Twin.
Watertight bulkheads: Fourteen.
Decks: Five.
Normal speed: 19.50 knots.
Officers and crew: 625.
Passenger accommodation: 523 first, 841 cabin, and 314 third class.
Maiden voyage for White Star Line: Southampton—New York, arriving on February 24, 1922.

Built for the North German Lloyd and was to be called *Columbus*. Launched as the *Columbus* on December 17, 1913. Construction was held up during World War I and she was not completed until 1920. Ceded to Great Britain in 1920 and sold to the White Star Line by the British Shipping Controller and renamed *Homeric*. Acquired by the Cunard Line on May 10, 1934 when the Cunard and White Star Lines merged to form the Cunard-White Star Line. Used solely for pleasure cruising while under Cunard ownership she was withdrawn from service in September 1935 and laid up at Ryde, England. Sold for scrapping in February 1936 and arrived at Inverkeithing, Scotland, in March.

Note: The *Homeric* was completed in 1920 by her German builders, but was altered considerably by the White Star Line and was completed by them in 1922 when she entered their service in February of that year. She was the largest ship in the world with twin-screws at the time of her construction and was notably one of the most plush liners of her time, of which the word plush had been a by-word with most of the White Star fleet.

I IVERNIA

Builder: Swan & Hunter Ltd, Wallsend-on-Tyne, England.

Completed: March 1900.

Gross tonnage: 14278.

Dimensions: 600ft × 65ft. Depth 42ft.

Engines: Four-cylinder quadruple expansion.

Screws: Twin.

Watertight bulkheads: Ten.

Decks: Four.

Normal speed: 16 knots.

Passenger accommodation: 164 first, 200 second, and 1366 third class of which 944 had staterooms.

Maiden voyage: Liverpool–New York on April 14, 1900.

Engaged in the Liverpool–Queenstown–Boston trade. The *Ivernia* struck Daunt's Rock outside of Queenstown on May 24, 1911, and did not resume service until October 17, 1911. The following month she was reallocated to the New York–Mediterranean trade after having been converted to a cabin-class ship while she had been laid up with new accommodation for 485 cabin- and 978 third-class passengers. Made some trips to Boston, but by March 1912 was scheduled permanently in the Line's Hungarian–American service from New York to Funchal, Naples, Palermo, Messina, Trieste and Fiume. Her fuel consumption was some 152 tons of coal per day and was one of the first vessels to feature the new thermotank ventilation system which enabled passengers to control the ventilation of air in their cabins. Requisitioned as a transport in September 1914 and was sunk by the U-47 58 miles off Cape Matapan, Greece on New Year's day 1917 with the loss of 200 of the 2800 troops on board and 22 crew members. The *Ivernia* had been under the command of Captain W.T. Turner, who also was in command when the *Lusitania* had been sunk in May 1915 off the Old Head of Kinsale, Ireland.

Sister ship: *Saxonia.*

I LACONIA

Builder: Swan, Hunter & Wigham Richardson Ltd, Newcastle-on-Tyne, England.
Completed: January 1912.
Gross tonnage: 18099.
Dimensions: 625ft × 71ft. Depth 40ft.
Engines: Two four-cylinder quadruple expansion.
Screws: Twin.
Watertight bulkheads: Ten.
Decks: Four.
Normal speed: 16 knots.
Passenger accommodation: 300 first, 350 second, and 2200 third class.
Maiden voyage: Liverpool–Queenstown–New York on January 20, 1912.

Employed in the Liverpool–Queenstown–Boston run during the summer months and in the New York–Mediterranean services throughout the winter months. The *Laconia* was the first Cunarder to be equipped with Frahm's anti-rolling tanks, the fore-runners of the modern gyro stabilisers. Refitted as an armed merchant cruiser in October 1914 until September 1916 when she was used as a baseship in the Rufuji river, Tanzania, Africa, for operations against the German cruiser *Konigsberg*. She returned to her regular Liverpool services on September 9, 1916, with a number of sailings to New York. Sunk by a German submarine 160 miles from Fastnet, Ireland, at 10pm on February 25, 1917, while on a commercial voyage, with a loss of 12 lives.
Sister ship: *Franconia.*

II LACONIA

Builder: Swan, Hunter & Wigham Richardson Ltd, Newcastle-on-Tyne, England.
Completed: January 1922.
Gross tonnage: 19695.
Dimensions: 624ft × 74ft. Depth 45ft.
Engines: Six steam turbines double-reduction geared.
Screws: Twin.
Watertight bulkheads: Ten.
Decks: Five.
Normal speed: 16 knots.
Passenger accommodation: 347 first, 350 second and 1500 third class.
Maiden voyage: Southampton–New York on May 25, 1922.

Engaged in the Liverpool–Cobh–New York and Boston services. She made some voyages from Hamburg to Southampton and New York in 1923, but reverted back to her original service. On January 24, 1938, the *Laconia* made a 52-day cruise from Liverpool covering 14108 miles and did much cruise work throughout the 'thirties. Converted to a liner-cruiser on September 2, 1939 and later did some trooping. On September 12, 1942 while 700 miles south-west of Freetown, Africa, she was hit by two torpedoes from the U-156. The first torpedo struck at 8.15pm and the second followed 15 minutes later. At 9.20pm the

Laconia foundered along with 1800 Italian prisoners of war and her British crew. 163 survived the ordeal and the German U-boats 506 and 507 later tarried with U-156 and collected the lifeboats into a group ordering them to remain where they were. The Germans later notified the Vichy French at Dakar, Senegal, where five days later the French cruiser *Gloire* arrived at the scene and took the survivors of British uniform to Casablanca, Morocco. The Italians had been taken by the U-506 earlier and not only gained their lives, but their freedom as well.
Sister ships: *Samaria* and *Scythia*.

LANCASTRIA

Builder: William Beardmore & Co Ltd, Glasgow, Scotland.
Completed: June 1922.
Gross tonnage: 16243.
Dimensions: 578ft × 70ft. Depth 43ft.
Engines: Six steam turbines double-reduction geared.
Screws: Twin.
Watertight bulkheads: Ten.
Decks: Five.
Normal speed: 16.50 knots.
Passenger accommodation: 235 first, 355 second, and 1256 third class.
Maiden voyage: Glasgow–Quebec–Montreal on June 13, 1922.

Built for the Anchor Line, but transferred to the Cunard Line while still on the stocks and christened *Tyrrhenia*. Renamed *Lancastria* in 1924. Engaged in the Liverpool–Quebec–Montreal run. In 1923 she was in the Hamburg–Southampton–New York service. Transferred to the London–Le Havre–Southampton–New York run in 1926 with a call at Plymouth eastbound. During the 'thirties she was used for cruising mostly in the Mediterranean. When World War II broke out she was cruising from New York to Nassau and made her last trip from New York on September 3, 1939. Requisitioned for troop work on March 5, 1940, *Lancastria* was to become one of the war's worst disasters. On June 17, 1940, the day France accepted Hitler's terms of surrender, *Lancastria* along with hundreds of other sea-worthy craft participated in the evacuation of troops at Dunkirk. As the *Lancastria* had finished with her complement of over 5500 men, women and children and her bunkers filled with fuel, she was attacked by seven or eight Junkers and Dorniers who dispersed four direct hits on her. The first went right through her funnel and exploded in the engine room. The others into her holds blowing out the sides of the ship to the sea. When the bombs hit with such simultaneous force, the *Lancastria* nearly jumped out of the water and foundered within 20 minutes. The appalling loss of life in this great disaster climbed way above the 3000 mark and would most probably have been less had the 1400 tons of fuel oil released after the bombing not covered the water's surface and prevented the swimmers from making the beach. Seven hours later at 11pm survivors were picked up by the anti-submarine trawler *Cambridgeshire* while under enemy fire. The sinking of the *Lancastria* had been so tragic that the news had been hushed almost throughout the war before it was released to the public.

LAURENTIC

Builder: Harland & Wolff Ltd, Belfast, Ireland.
Completed: November 1927.
Gross tonnage: 18724.
Dimensions: 603ft × 75ft. Depth 41ft.
Engines: Two four-cylinder triple expansion engines and one low-pressure turbine.
Screws: Triple.
Decks: Five.
Normal speed: 16.50 knots.
Maiden voyage for Cunard Line: Liverpool —Quebec—Montreal, arriving on July 14, 1934.

Built for the White Star Line and passed on to Cunard Line ownership on May 10, 1934 when the two companies merged. Used solely for pleasure cruising while under Cunard ownership after having made only two trips to Canada and laid up in the River Fal, England. Sent cruising once again when on the night of August 18, 1935, the Blue Star liner *Napier Star* rammed into the *Laurentic* off the Skerries in the Irish Sea during a fog. The *Napier Star* crashed into her starboard bow and killed six of the *Laurentic*'s crew. She

was subsequently laid up at Millbrook, Southampton, in December 1935, but did some troop work to Israel in September 1936. Laid up once again in April 1938 in the River Fal until she was commissioned as an armed merchant cruiser on August 24, 1939, and sunk by submarine U-99 off Bloody Foreland, Ireland, on November 4, 1940. The first torpedo struck the *Laurentic* at 9.50pm on the night of the 3rd sinking her 2 hours later. She was the last of the coal-firing liners and the last to be driven by reciprocating machinery.

LUCANIA

Builder: Fairfield Shipbuilding & Engineering Co Ltd, Glasgow, Scotland.
Completed: July 1893.
Gross tonnage: 12952.
Dimensions: 622ft × 65ft. Depth 38ft.
Engines: Two three-cylinder triple expansion.
Screws: Twin.
Watertight bulkheads: Twelve.
Decks: Three.
Normal speed: 22 knots.
Officers and crew: 415.
Passenger accommodation: 526 first, 280 second and 1000 steerage.
Maiden voyage: Liverpool—New York on September 2, 1893.
Last voyage for Cunard Line: New York—Queenstown—Liverpool on July 7, 1909.

Employed in the Liverpool—Queenstown—New York run. The *Lucania* won the Blue Riband from her sister *Campania* in May 1894 by making the run from Sandy Hook to Queenstown in 5 days, 8 hours and 38 minutes at a speed of 21.95 knots. On October 10, 1903, she became well known by being the first liner in touch with the Marconi stations at Cape Breton, Nova Scotia, and Poldhu, England, by wireless, thus marking a new era in oceanic journalism with the new 'Cunard's Daily Bulletin' which recorded the most important events on both sides of the Atlantic. Damaged extensively by fire at Huskisson dock at Liverpool on August 14, 1909, and was subsequently sold to Wards of Sheffield for scrap at Swansea, Wales. She ran to the shipbreaker's yard at a speed of 17 knots and was completely dismantled by 1910.
Sister ship: *Campania*.

LUSITANIA

Builder: John Brown & Co Ltd, Clydebank, Glasgow, Scotland.
Completed: August 1907.
Gross tonnage: 30396.
Dimensions: 790ft × 88ft. Depth 61ft.
Engines: Four direct-action Parson steam turbines; two high pressure and two low pressure.
Screws: Quadruple.
Watertight bulkheads: Eleven.
Decks: Six.
Normal speed: 24.50 knots.
Officers and crew: 1800.
Passenger accommodation: 563 first, 464 second and 1138 third class.
Maiden voyage: Liverpool–Queenstown–New York on September 7, 1907.

Engaged in the Liverpool–Queenstown–New York service. She recaptured the Blue Riband from the North German Lloyd's *Kaiser Wilhelm II* on her second voyage in October 1907 by making the run from Queenstown to Sandy Hook in 4 days, 19 hours and 52 minutes at a speed of 23.99 knots. To attain her high speed the *Lusitania* consumed 850 tons of coal every 24 hours. In 1914 she was commissioned by the Admiralty but was soon released back to her owners. On May 1, 1915 the *Lusitania* sailed out of New York on her eastbound voyage with a complement of over 2000 passengers and crew. At 2.10pm on May 7, 1915 while off the Old Head of Kinsale, Ireland, she was hit without warning by two torpedoes from the German U-20. The first hit between the first and second funnels and the second followed almost

immediately, the *Lusitania* gave a list of 15 degrees to starboard and made it impossible to launch the port-side lifeboats. With her sides open to the sea the *Lusitania* sank within 18 minutes by the head with the appalling loss of 1198 lives of which 124 were Americans. An attempt to salve the gold cargo on board was made by the salvage ship *Orphir* in October 1935, but being that she lay some 60 fathoms below it was soon abandoned. On November 6, 1935, a memorial was held on board the *Orphir* over the scene of the wreck with some of the survivors attending the service. The *Lusitania* had been the first quadruple-screw ship ever built and was one of the most disastrous tragedies of World War I. The *Lusitania* will long be remembered.
Sister ship: *Mauretania.*

MAJESTIC

Builder: Blohm & Voss, Hamburg, Germany.
Completed: March 1922.
Gross tonnage: 56599.
Dimensions: 956ft × 100ft. Depth 58ft.
Engines: Eight direct-action Parson turbines.
Screws: Quadruple.
Watertight bulkheads: Eleven.
Decks: Seven.
Normal speed: 23.50 knots.
Passenger accommodation: 700 first, 545 second and 850 third class.
Maiden voyage: Southampton–Cherbourg–New York on July 4, 1934.

Built jointly for the Cunard & White Star Lines and launched as the *Bismarck* on June 20, 1914 for the Hamburg–America Line. Construction was held up during World War I and she was not completed until March 1922. She had, meanwhile, been ceded to Britain in 1919 under the treaty of Versailles and was sold by the British Shipping Controller to a joint ownership between the Cunard and White Star Lines and renamed *Majestic*. Later passed on to complete White Star ownership but later under the Cunard-White Star Line when the two companies merged on May 10, 1934. The Cunard Line had held 62 per cent of the stock in the new company. Employed in the Southampton–Cherbourg–New York run for Cunard-White Star Line. The *Majestic* was well known as the 'Queen of the Western Ocean' and

was the largest ship afloat when built up until the French Line's *Normandie*. Her funnels were 180ft high from the furnace bars and she was the first liner to show sound motion pictures. Made her last transatlantic voyage for the Line on February 22, 1936, from New York to Southampton, via Cherbourg. Laid up in March 1936 and sold to T. W. Ward on May 15, 1936, for the sum of £115000 and was, in turn resold to the Admiralty for conversion to a boys' training ship and renamed *Caledonia* in 1937. Gutted by fire and sank at Rosyth, Scotland, on September 29, 1939. Sold once again to Ward's in March 1940 and refloated on July 17, 1943, and taken to Inverkeithing, Scotland, for breaking up. She was the largest ship yet sold for scrap.

I MAURETANIA

Builder: Swan, Hunter & Wigham Richardson Ltd, Wallsend-on-Tyne, England.
Completed: October 1907.
Gross tonnage: 30696.
Dimensions: 790ft × 88ft. Depth 61ft.
Engines: Four direct-action Parson steam turbines; two high pressure and two low pressure.
Screws: Quadruple.
Watertight bulkheads: Eleven.
Decks: Six.
Normal speed: 25.50 knots. (Attained a speed of 27.04 knots on her trial runs.)
Officers and crew: 812.
Passenger accommodation: 563 first, 464 second, and 1138 third class.
Maiden voyage: Liverpool—Queenstown—New York on November 16, 1907.

In November 1907 she won the Blue Riband from her sister *Lusitania* by making the run from Ambrose Lighthouse to Queenstown in 4 days, 22 hours and 29 minutes at a speed of 23.69 knots. She lost the title back to her sister, but regained it permanently in July 1909 eastbound with a crossing of 4 days, 17 hours and 20 minutes at a speed of 25.89 knots. Commissioned as a transport in August 1914 and was later used as a hospital ship. Laid up at Greenock, Scotland, between 1916 and 1917 and transported American troops in late 1917. Decommissioned in May 1919 and resumed services on June 27, 1919, from Southampton to New York. Damaged by fire at Southampton on July 25, 1921, she was repaired and fitted for oil fuel. Re-entered service on March 25, 1922, from Southampton to Cherbourg and New York with a call at Plymouth eastbound. In 1931 her hull was painted white and she was sent cruising. The following year she

made only five transatlantic voyages. On September 26, 1934, the day the *Queen Mary* was launched, the *Mauretania* made her last voyage from New York—Plymouth—Cherbourg—Southampton and was withdrawn from service in October. Sold to Metal Industries on April 2 1935, for scrapping. The *Mauretania* left Southampton on July 1, 1935, for Rosyth, Scotland, to be broken up — her departure being broadcast by radio. The *Mauretania* had been, through the years, the most popular ship among the general public to sail on the North Atlantic Ferry. She had held the Blue Riband for 22 years; her speed increasing as she aged with a record of 27.65 knots in 1929. She was well known as 'The Grand Old Lady'. The *Mauretania* exercised an eminence that no other liner could ever assume since her long mourned absence. It was a shame she could not have had a more regal death.
Sister ship: *Lusitania*.

II MAURETANIA

Builder: Cammell, Laird & Co Ltd, Birkenhead, England.
Completed: June 1939.
Gross tonnage: 35655.
Dimensions: 772ft × 54ft. Depth 54ft.
Engines: Six steam turbines, single-reduction geared.
Screws: Twin.
Decks: Six.
Normal speed: 23 knots.
Officers and crew: 593.
Passenger accommodation: 475 first, 390 cabin, and 304 tourist class.
Maiden voyage: Liverpool–New York on June 19, 1939.
Last voyage: a cruise from New York to the Mediterranean on September 15, 1965.

She made only four trips to New York and was laid up at New York from December 16, 1939, until she was requisitioned for troop work on March 1, 1940. Left New York on March 20, 1940, for Sydney, Australia, via Balboa and Honolulu. After carrying over 350000 troops and steaming 542000 miles on 48 voyages she arrived at Liverpool on May 30, 1945, completing her war services. Overhauled between September 1946 and April 1947 at Birkenhead and re-entered service on April 26, 1947, from Liverpool to New York. Engaged in the Southampton–Le Havre–Cobh–New York service with cruises during the off season from New York. She was given full air-conditioning in 1957. In 1962 her hull was painted to a light green hue and made an attempt to break into the passenger trade from New York to the Mediterranean. This proved to be unsuccessful and she was used more extensively for cruise purposes from out of New York and Southampton. Withdrawn from service on November 10, 1965, upon her arrival at Southampton. Sold for scrap at Inverkeithing, Scotland, arriving on November 23. She was broken up by March 1966.

MEDIA

Builder: John Brown & Co Ltd, Clydebank, Glasgow, Scotland.
Completed: August 1947.
Gross tonnage: 12345.
Dimensions: 531ft × 70ft. Depth 46ft.
Engines: Four steam turbines double-reduction geared.
Screws: Twin.
Watertight bulkheads: Ten.

Decks: Four.
Normal speed: 18 knots.
Officers and crew: 189.
Cargo capacity: 422430 cubic feet of general and insulated space.
Passenger accommodation: 251 first class passengers.
Maiden voyage: Mersey—New York on August 20, 1947.
Last voyage for Cunard Line: New York—Liverpool on September 22, 1961.

Employed in the Liverpool—New York run with an occasional call at Cobh or Greenock eastbound. Equipped with motion stabilisers and all public rooms are air-conditioned. Sold to the Cogedar Line in October 1961 and renamed *Flavia*. Presently in their service.
Sister ship: *Parthia*.

OLYMPIC

Builder: Harland & Wolff Ltd, Belfast, Ireland.
Completed: June 1911.
Gross tonnage: 44439.
Dimensions: 882ft × 92ft. Depth 59ft.
Engines: Two four-cylinder triple-expansion engines and one low-pressure turbine.
Screws: Triple.
Watertight bulkheads: Fifteen.
Decks: Seven.
Normal speed: 21.50 knots.
Officers and crew: 853.
Passenger accommodation: 2021 in first, tourist and third class.
Maiden voyage: Southampton–Cherbourg–New York in 1934.

Built for the White Star Line. Transferred to the Cunard Line on May 10, 1934 when the two companies amalgamated. Employed mostly as a cruise ship while under Cunard·White Star with some voyages to New York. On May 16, 1934, the Olympic rammed and sunk the Nantucket lightship in a dense fog off the New England coast of America. All seven of the lightship's crew were lost and the United States Government brought suit against the Line for a half million dollars. Withdrawn in March 1935 and sold to John Jarvis shipbreakers in September. The Olympic left Southampton for the last time on October 11, 1935, and sailed for the scrapyard at Jarrow, England.
Sister ship: Titanic.

II PARTHIA

Builder: Harland & Wolff Ltd, Belfast, Ireland.
Completed: April 1948.
Gross tonnage: 13362.
Dimensions: 531ft × 70ft. Depth 46ft.
Engines: Four steam turbines double-reduction geared.
Screws: Twin.
Watertight bulkheads: Ten.
Decks: Four.
Normal speed: 18 knots.
Officers and crew: 189.
Cargo capacity: 422430 cubic feet of general and insulated space.
Passenger accommodation: 251 first class passengers.
Maiden voyage: Liverpool–New York on April 10, 1948.
Last voyage for Cunard Line: Liverpool–New York, arriving on September 30, 1961.

Employed in the Liverpool–New York run with an occasional call at Cobh or Greenock eastbound. Equipped with motion stabilisers and all public rooms are air-conditioned. Sold to the New Zealand Shipping Co on November 1, 1961, and renamed *Remuera*. Resold to the Eastern & Australian Steamship Co in January 1965 and renamed *Aramac*. Sold to the Chin Ho Fa Steel & Iron Co Ltd in Taiwan in November 1969 for scrapping and delivered on November 22, 1969. Broken up between March 5 and May 31, 1970.
Sister ship: *Media.*

QUEEN ELIZABETH

Builder: John Brown & Co Ltd, Clydebank,
   Glasgow, Scotland.
Completed: February 1940.
Gross tonnage: 82998.
Dimensions: 1031ft × 119ft. Depth 74ft.
Engines: Sixteen steam turbines single-reduc-
   tion geared.
Screws: Quadruple.
Watertight bulkheads: Fifteen.
Decks: Ten.
Normal speed: 29 knots.
Officers and crew: 1296.
Passenger accommodation: 882 first, 668
   cabin and 798 tourist class.
Maiden voyage: Southampton–New York on
   October 16, 1946.

The *Queen Elizabeth* is the largest ship in the world and has a promenade deck that is 724ft long. Her forward funnel is 71ft high and each pro-peller weighs 32 tons, and anchors of 16 tons. Employed in the Southampton–Cherbourg–New York run with a call at Plymouth eastbound and some cruising. She was fitted with twin stabilisers in March 1955. Operating at a loss during the late 'sixties the Cunard Line duly decided to sell the *Queen Elizabeth* to the city of Fort Lauderdale, Florida and the contract was enacted on April 5, 1968. The *Elizabeth* left berth number 107 at Southampton on her last voyage for her new home in Florida on November 29, 1968. She was then converted, like her running mate the *Queen Mary*, into an hotel and nightclub. Throughout her career she made 907 Atlantic crossings; covered over 3470000 miles and carried more than 2300000 passengers excluding her war service Affirmed the largest ship the world had ever seen she lacked the graceful lines of the lesser-sized liners. Since her sale to the city of Fort Lauderdale she has not proven a success and has been making some trips under the name of *Seawise University* after her sale to Mr C. Y. Tung in 1970 as a floating University. On January 9, 1972, fire broke out while she was being renovated in Hong Kong. The vessel was engulfed by flames and capsized at noon the following day.

Note: The *Queen Elizabeth* was secretly crossed to New York from the Clyde on February 27, 1940, to be fitted out as a transport with accommoda-tion for almost 20000 armed men. Decommis-sioned on March 6, 1946, after having steamed 492635 miles and carrying 811324 service per-sonnel. Overhauled at John Brown's after the war.

QUEEN ELIZABETH 2

Builder: John Brown & Co Ltd, Upper Clyde, Glasgow, Scotland.
Completed: April 1969.
Gross tonnage: 65863.
Dimensions: 963ft × 105ft. Depth 74ft.
Engines: Four steam turbines double-reduction geared.
Screws: Twin.
Collision bulkhead: One.
Watertight bulkheads: Fourteen.
Decks: Seven.
Normal speed: 28.50 knots.
Officers and crew: 906.
Passenger accommodation: 564 first and 1979 tourist class. (Accommodations are limited to 1400 when in cruise service.)
Maiden voyage: Southampton–Le Havre–Cobh–New York on May 2, 1969.

Employed in the Southampton–Le Havre–New York run with a call at Cobh eastbound and cruising. The *Queen Elizabeth 2* is built with a bulbous bow and is auxiliary equipped with two Stone Kamewa bow thrusters athwartship. Fully air-conditioned and fitted with Denny-Brown motion stabilisers. Her promenade deck is 750ft long. She has ten lounges; eleven bars and a theatre seating 530 persons. With all these comforts and the new interior and exterior modes of the *Queen Elizabeth 2* we only hope the passenger can still remember he is on a ship. She is the largest twin-screw vessel and is formally known as the *QE2*. She is the Cunard Line's flagship and is presently in service. *(See Notes on p. 223.)*

QUEEN MARY

Builder: John Brown & Co Ltd, Clydebank, Glasgow, Scotland.

Completed: May 1936. (She was laid down on December 27, 1930. Work was suspended from December 1931 until April 1934 due to the depression and she was not completed until May 1936.)

Gross tonnage: 81237.

Dimensions: 1020ft × 119ft. Depth 74ft.

Engines: Sixteen steam turbines single-reduction geared.

Screws: Quadruple.

Watertight bulkheads: Eighteen.

Decks: Ten.

Normal speed: 30 knots. (Attained a speed of 32.84 knots on her trials.)

Officers and crew: 1285.

Passenger accommodation: 711 first, 707 cabin and 577 tourist class.

Maiden voyage: Southampton–Cherbourg–New York on May 27, 1936.

On her sixth voyage out the *Queen Mary* won the Blue Riband from the French Line's *Normandie* by making the run from Bishop Rock to Ambrose Lighthouse in 4 days, 27 minutes at a speed of 30.14 knots. She soon lost the title back to the *Normandie* the following year, but recovered it in 1938 with an outward crossing of 3 days, 21 hours and 48 minutes at a speed of 30.99 knots. Commissioned as a transport on March 1, 1940, while at New York after being laid up since the outbreak of war. Fitted out at Sydney, Australia, and made her first voyage from there on May 5, 1940. On October 2, 1942, the anti-aircraft cruiser *Curaçao* attempted to clear the bow of the *Queen Mary* while in convoy, but failed and the *Queen* severed her stern like a knife cutting through butter and killing 338 of the men on board while just north of Bloody Foreland, Ireland. On September 29, 1946, the *Queen Mary* arrived at Southampton from Halifax on her last trooping voyage and a few days later was sent to John Brown's for reconversion to a passenger ship. Almost a year later she commenced her first post-war sailing from Southampton to Cherbourg and New York on July 31, 1947. The *Queen Mary* was engaged in the Southampton –Cherbourg–New York service with a call at Plymouth eastbound. Some of the *Queen's* outstanding features are her promenade deck which is 750ft long; a rudder weighing some 140 tons and her anchors each of 16 tons with 165 fathoms of chain cable. Her after funnel is 78ft above the boat deck. In 1958 she was fitted with motion stabilisers. Operating at a loss of about $2 million a year in the latter part of her life, the Cunard Line decided to sell her to the highest bidder in May 1967 rather than send her to the scrapyards. On August 18, 1967, the transaction was enacted with the City of Long Beach, California, for a consideration of $3450000. Arriving at Southampton on September 27, 1967, completing her thousandth and last voyage for the Cunard Line. Refitted over a period of four years when she opened for business as a maritime museum and hotel and convention centre on May 10, 1971. The *Queen Mary* is now enjoying a long rest after her many years of service.

ROYAL GEORGE

Builder: Fairfield Shipbuilding & Engineering Co Ltd, Glasgow, Scotland.
Completed: November 1907.
Gross tonnage: 11146.
Dimensions: 541ft × 60ft. Depth 27ft.
Engines: Three direct action steam turbines.
Screws: Triple.
Normal speed: 18 knots.
Passenger accommodation: 350 second and 110 saloon.
Maiden voyage: Liverpool–New York on February 8, 1919.

Built for the Egyptian Mail Steamship & Engineering Co, and christened *Heliopolis*. Sold to the Royal Line in 1910 and renamed *Royal George*. Resold to Cunard Line in February 1919. Engaged in the Liverpool–New York run until August 14, 1919, when she was re-routed to work out of Southampton. She was later used as a depot ship at Cherbourg, France for a time, at the conclusion of her services on her last voyage from New York to Southampton on June 17, 1920. Laid up at Falmouth, England, in 1921. The *Royal George* had been purchased to make up for the Line's loss in tonnage during World War I. She had acquired the name of 'Rolling George' because of her exceedingly unsteadiness at sea. Sold for scrap at Wilhelmshaven, Germany, in September 1922.

II SAMARIA

Builder: Cammell, Laird & Co Ltd, Birkenhead, England.
Completed: August 1921.
Gross tonnage: 19848.
Dimensions: 624ft × 74ft. Depth 45ft.
Engines: Six steam turbines double-reduction geared.
Screws: Twin.
Watertight bulkheads: Ten.
Decks: Five.
Normal speed: 16 knots.
Officers and crew: 434.
Passenger accommodation: 248 first and 641 tourist class.
Maiden voyage: Liverpool–Boston on April 19, 1922.

Engaged in the Liverpool–Queenstown–New York and Boston services and some cruising. In 1934 she made ten consecutive cruises out of London. Requisitioned for troop work in 1941 and was decommissioned in August 1948 when she carried Canadian troops and their families from Cuxhaven and Le Havre to Quebec or Halifax in September 1948. She then worked out of London to Quebec and Montreal in 1950 and was re-routed to her home port of Liverpool to Quebec on June 14, 1951, after being refitted in the autumn of 1950.

Placed in the Southampton–Le Havre–Quebec run on July 12, 1951. The *Samaria* ran aground just below Quebec in 1952, but was refloated without difficulty. On June 15, 1953, she represented the Cunard Line at the Coronation Review at Spithead, England and commenced her last voyage Quebec–Le Havre–Southampton on November 23, 1955. Sold for scrap at Inverkeithing, Scotland, in January 1956.
Sister ships: *Laconia* and *Scythia*.

1 SAXONIA

Builder: John Brown & Co Ltd, Clydebank, Glasgow, Scotland.
Completed: April 1900.
Gross tonnage: 14197.
Dimensions: 600ft × 64ft. Depth 42ft.
Engines: Two four-cylinder quadruple expansion.
Screws: Twin.
Watertight bulkheads: Ten.
Decks: Four.
Normal speed: 16 knots.
Passenger accommodation: 485 cabin and 978 third class.
Maiden voyage: Liverpool–Boston on May 22, 1900.

Engaged in the Liverpool–Queenstown–Boston run and from New York to the Mediterranean since November 1909 throughout the winter season returning to the Boston service in the summer. By February 1912 she had been scheduled permanently in the Line's Hungarian–American service from New York to Funchal, Naples, Palermo, Messina, Trieste and Fiume. The *Saxonia's* funnel was 106ft high from the upper-most deck and she had a coal capacity of 1430 tons. Requisitioned for troop work in September 1914 until May 1, 1915, when she re-entered service from Liverpool to New York. She was then withdrawn for a time and resumed sailings on January 25, 1919. Reallocated to the London–New York run on May 14, 1919, and later to the New York–Hamburg route on April 1920. Sold to Dutch shipbreakers in March 1925.
Sister ship: *Ivernia.*

II SCYTHIA

Builder: Vickers Ltd, Barrow-in-Furness, England. (*Scythia* was completed at Rotterdam, Holland owing to a labour strike in England.)
Completed: December 1920.
Gross tonnage: 19930.
Dimensions: 624ft × 74ft. Depth 45ft.
Engines: Six steam turbines double-reduction geared.
Screws: Twin.
Watertight bulkheads: Ten.
Decks: Five.
Normal speed: 16 knots.
Officers and crew: 434.
Passenger accommodation: 248 first and 630 tourist class.
Maiden voyage: Liverpool–New York on August 20, 1921.

Engaged in the Liverpool–Queenstown–New York and Boston services with some cruising. Requisitioned for troop service on August 27, 1939 and was almost sunk by an aerial torpedo in Algiers harbour in November 1942. Damaged, she was towed to Gibraltar for repairs and later made it to New York on June 9, 1943, for further repairs lasting over a period of ten weeks. She then transported American troops to Britain in September and October of 1943. After being decommissioned in September 1948 she carried displaced persons from Cuxhaven and Le Havre to Quebec or Halifax on ten voyages which terminated in October 1949. Refitted in November of that year and re-entered service from Liverpool to Quebec on August 17, 1950, and from London to Quebec and Montreal on September 14, 1950. On April 10, 1951, she was re-routed to sail from Southampton to Le Havre and Quebec with some voyages to New York on occasion. The *Scythia* had the misfortune of colliding with the Candian collier *Wabana* 35 miles south of St'Anne de Montes in the St Lawrence on June 5, 1952. The *Scythia* sheered off 32ft of the *Wabana*'s starboard side while travelling at a speed of 14 knots. There was no loss of life, but both vessels were found at fault when a formal investigation revealed that neither had made proper and diligent use of their radar. She commenced her last voyage for the Line on October 5, 1957, from Liverpool to Cobh and New York. She was then chartered by the Canadian Government for two voyages carrying Canadian service personnel from Rotterdam to Quebec on November 28, 1957, and arrived at Southampton on December 12 for the last time. Withdrawn from service in December and left for the scrapyard at Inverkeithing, Scotland, on January 1, 1958.
Sister ships: *Laconia* and *Samaria*.

SLAVONIA

Builder: James Laing & Sons Ltd, Sunderland, England.
Completed: May 1903.
Gross tonnage: 10606.
Dimensions: 526ft × 59ft. Depth 33ft.
Engines: Two three-cylinder tripple expansion.
Watertight bulkheads: Eight.
Decks: Three.
Normal speed: 13.50 knots.
Passenger accommodation: 40 saloon and 800 steerage.
Maiden voyage: Sunderland—Trieste on March 17, 1904.

Engaged in the New York—Gibraltar—Naples—Palermo—Messina—Trieste—Fiume run. The *Slavonia* made some Liverpool—Fiume trips after her yearly drydocking and was wrecked at Flores island in the Azores on June 10, 1909, with no loss of life.
Sister ship: *Pannonia*.

II SYLVANIA

Builder: John Brown & Co Ltd, Clydebank,
 Glasgow, Scotland.
Completed: June 1957.
Gross tonnage: 22017.
Dimensions: 608ft × 80ft. Depth 46ft.
Engines: Four steam turbines double-reduction
 geared.
Screws: Twin.
Collision bulkhead: One.
Watertight bulkheads: Nine.
Decks: Five.
Normal speed: 20 knots.
Officers and crew: 460.
Passenger accommodation: 172 first and 724
 tourist class. (Accommodations are combined
 into one class when pleasure-cruising.)
Maiden voyage: Greenock–Quebec–Montreal
 on June 5, 1957.

Engaged in the Liverpool–Greenock–Quebec–Montreal run. Reallocated to the Liverpool–Cobh–New York service in 1961 with some cruising. In February 1965 the *Sylvania* made a Mediterranean cruise which was the first such cruise for Cunard since January 1939. In 1967 she was based at Gibraltar for a series of cruises to the Mediterranean. She is equipped with motion stabilisers and all public rooms are air-conditioned. *Sylvania* made her last voyage for Cunard on December 12, 1967, after a short life of only ten years with the Line. Sold to the Airwind Corporation in 1968 and renamed *Fairwind.* Currently in their service under the Liberian flag.
Sister ships: *Carinthia, Carmania,* and *Franconia.*

ULTONIA

Builder: Swan & Hunter Ltd, Wallsend-on-Tyne, England.
Completed: October 1898.
Gross tonnage: 10402.
Dimensions: 513ft × 57ft. Depth 34ft.
Engines: Two three-cylinder triple expansion engines.
Screws: Twin.
Watertight bulkheads: Eight.
Decks: Three.
Normal speed: 13 knots.
Maiden voyage: Liverpool—Boston on February 28, 1899.

Built for the British India Steam Navigation Co and was to be called *Yamuna*. Sold to the Cunard Line after launching and renamed *Ultonia*. Engaged in the Liverpool—Queenstown—Boston trade with an occasional trip to New York. In May 1904 she was reallocated to the New York—Gibraltar—Naples—Palermo—Messina—Trieste—Fiume service on the company's Hungarian–American Line. Between 1911 and 1912 she made a few trips to Boston and Canada and in April 1912 was converted from a three-class ship to cabin and third re-entering her regular service on September 24, 1912, with still a few trips from London to Southampton, Quebec and Montreal. Requisitioned for war services in September 1914 until December 8, 1916, when she resumed commercial sailings from London to New York. Sunk by a German submarine 350 miles south-west of Land's End, England on June 27, 1917, with the loss of one life.

FRENCH LINE

II ANTILLES

Builder: Arsenal de Brest, Brest, France.
Completed: 1952.
Gross tonnage: 19828.
Dimensions: 599ft × 80ft. Depth 46ft.
Engines: Eight steam turbines double-reduction geared.
Screws: Twin.
Decks: Five.
Normal speed: 23 knots.
Passenger accommodation: 404 first, 285 cabin and 89 tourist class.
Maiden voyage: Le Havre—West Indies in May 1953.

Employed in the Le Havre—Southampton—West Indies trade. She is fully air-conditioned and is equipped with motion stabilisers. The *Antilles* has on occasion made some voyages to New York and cruising. On the evening of January 8, 1971, at approximately 5pm the *Antilles* went aground on an uncharted submerged reef a half mile off the island of Mustique in the Caribbean and burst into flames when a fuel tank had burst after the collision creating an onrush of oil into the boiler room. At one time the fire-fighting crew seemed to have had the fire under control, but the fervour of the flames grew with such intensity that it became impossible to extinguish the inferno. At 5.22pm the *Antilles'* call of distress was picked up at the nearby island of Barbados where merchant vessels were sent to pick up the passengers and crew of the stricken liner. Of 635 passengers and crew all were disembarked safely at Mustique by the French Line's 'Banana' boat *Point Allegre*, and the *Suffren* plus other small craft, not to mention the ship's own life-saving apparatus. Some 500 passengers were later picked up at Mustique by the Cunard Line's *Queen Elizabeth 2* and brought to the island of Barbados where they were able to make other arrangements for their destinations. The last report of the *Antilles'* fate was the following day when she had rolled over on her side, still engulfed in flames. She was designated a total loss and had been valued at some $14.4 million. A terrible misfortune to the French Line and to the many travellers who came to know this lovely ship. It was a godsend that all the people aboard that fatal night disembarked with their lives. Plans to salvage the hulk were abandoned on January 18, 1971 when she broke in half and became a total loss.
Sister ship: *Flandre*.
(See Notes on p. 223.)

BRETAGNE

Builder: Barclay, Curle & Co Ltd, Glasgow, Scotland.
Completed: September 1922.
Gross tonnage: 10108.
Dimensions: 472ft × 59ft. Depth 45ft.
Engines: Four Curtiss steam turbines double-reduction geared.
Screws: Twin.
Watertight bulkheads: Seven.
Decks: Four.
Normal speed: 14.50 knots.
Passenger accommodation: 440 in a single first-class capacity.

Built for the Royal Holland Lloyd and christened *Flandria*. Sold to the French Line in 1937 and renamed *Bretagne*. Engaged in the St. Nazaire—Colon —Mexico—West Indies trade and later worked out of Le Havre—English ports—West Indies service. The *Bretagne*'s tonnage was later reduced to 8119 gross tons and she was sunk by a submarine on October 14, 1939, while *en route* to England.

CHAMPLAIN

Builder: Chantiers & Ateliers de St. Nazaire,
Penhoet, France.
Completed: 1932.
Gross tonnage: 28124.
Dimensions: 645ft × 83ft. Depth 46ft.
Engines: Six Parson steam turbines single-
reduction geared.
Screws: Twin.
Decks: Five.
Normal speed: 20 knots.
Officers and crew: 559.
Passenger accommodation: 548 cabin, 318
tourist and 134 third class.
Maiden voyage: Le Havre–New York on
June 18, 1932.

Engaged in the Le Havre–Southampton–New York service calling at Plymouth eastbound and cruising during the off seasonal months. The *Champlain* had a promenade deck 350ft long and a dining room two decks high and 65ft long. Struck an acoustic mine off La Pallice, France, on June 17, 1940, and sank within a quarter of an hour while she had been working from Bordeaux since the German invasion. The *Champlain* lived a regretfully short time for a liner as did her consorts *Lafayette* and *Normandie*.

CHICAGO

Builder: Chantiers de L'Atlantique de St.Nazaire, Penhoet, France.
Completed: 1908.
Gross tonnage: 10502.
Dimensions: 508ft × 58ft. Depth 39ft.
Engines: Two three-cylinder triple expansion.
Screws: Twin.
Watertight bulkheads: Fourteen.
Decks: Four.
Normal speed: 15.50 knots.
Passenger accommodation: 292 second and 1158 steerage.
Maiden voyage: Le Havre–New York on May 30, 1908.

Engaged in the Bordeaux–New York service from 1924 until 1928 when she was reconstructed and her name changed to *Guadeloupe* with a new service from St. Nazaire to Antilles and the West Indies. Sold for scrap at St. Nazaire, France, in 1936 and was broken up by 1937.

COLOMBIE

Builder: Ateliers & Chantiers de France, Dunkirk, France.
Completed: 1931.
Gross tonnage: 12803.
Dimensions: 509ft × 67ft. Depth 42ft.
Engines: Six steam turbines, single-reduction geared.
Screws: Twin.
Decks: Five.
Normal speed: 16 knots.
Passenger accommodation: 192 first, 140 cabin and 246 tourist class.
Maiden voyage: Le Havre–Colon–West Indies on November 1, 1931.

Employed in the Le Havre–English ports–Côte Ferme–Cristobal service. Commissioned as a transport in 1939 and seized by the United States at Martinique, West Indies in 1942 and utilised as a transport. In 1946 she was used as a hospital ship under the name of *Aleda E. Lutz*. Returned to the French Line in the same year and recovered her original name and resumed regular sailings. Withdrawn in late 1948 to undergo a complete reconstruction lasting two years at Flushing, Netherlands. She emerged as a single-funnelled ship, which replaced her former two, and many interior

modifications. Resumed service on October 12 1950, in the Le Havre–Southampton–Pointe à Piere–Roseau–Fort de France–St. Lucia–Trinidad–Barbados westbound and Barbados–Fort de France–Pointe à Piere–Plymouth–Le Havre eastbound. Engaged in this route until December 1962 when she was settled to permanent cruising to the Antilles. Sold to the Typaldos Lines in March 1964 and renamed *Atlantic*; *Atlantica*. Sold to Messrs Nemo A.E. at Perama, Greece, for scrap in 1970 and broken up by September 1970.

CUBA

Builder: Swan, Hunter & Wigham Richardson Ltd, Wallsend-on-Tyne, England.
Completed: 1923.
Gross tonnage: 11337.
Dimensions: 495ft × 62ft. Depth 35ft.
Engines: Four Rateau steam turbines double-reduction geared.
Screws: Twin.
Decks: Four.
Normal speed: 16 knots.
Passenger accommodation: 448 in a single first-class capacity.
Maiden voyage: St. Nazaire–Havana–Vera Cruz in May 1923.

Engaged in the St. Nazaire–Vera Cruz–West Indies–Central American trade. Taken over by the British Ministry of War in December 1941 and converted to a transport and managed by the Cunard Line. Sunk in the English Channel on April 6, 1945, while *en route* to Le Havre.

I DE GRASSE

Builder: Cammell, Laird & Co Ltd, Birkenhead, England.
Completed: 1924.
Gross tonnage: 19665.
Dimensions: 572ft × 71ft. Depth 42ft.
Engines: Four steam turbines single-reduction geared.
Screws: Twin.
Watertight bulkheads: Twelve.
Decks: Five.
Normal speed: 16.50 knots.
Passenger accommodation: 536 cabin and 410 tourist class.
Maiden voyage: Le Havre–New York on August 21, 1924.

The *De Grasse* was laid down in 1918 but work was suspended until 1923 because of the war. She was later towed to St. Nazaire for completion when a British labour dispute threatened further delay. Ordered as *Suffren*, but altered to *De Grasse* when the French Line purchased the Hamburg-America liner *Bluecher* and gave her the name of *Suffren* in 1923. Engaged in the Le Havre–New York trade with a call at Plymouth eastbound. During the mid 'thirties she did some work in the Mediterranean area and was transferred to the Bordeaux–New York run in 1937. Withdrawn from service in 1940 and sunk by German gunfire at Bordeaux on

August 30, 1944. Refloated on August 30, 1945, and reconditioned and replacement of her former two stacks by a single squat type. *De Grasse* inaugurated the Line's first voyage after the war and sailed from Le Havre to New York on July 12, 1947, and now called at Southampton east- and westbound. Reallocated to the West Indies service on April 24, 1952, out of Le Havre and was sold to the Canadian-Pacific Line in February 1953 to become the *Empress of Australia*. Resold to the Grimaldi-Siosa Line in February 1956 and renamed *Venezuela*. Stranded in March 1962 and broken up in Italy in December 1962.

II   DE GRASSE

Builder: Swan, Hunter & Wigham Richardson
   Ltd, Wallsend-on-Tyne, England.
Completed: May 1956.
Gross tonnage: 18739.
Dimensions: 578ft × 72ft. Depth 47ft.
Engines: Two eight-cylinder, two-stroke,
   double-acting diesel.
Screws: Twin.
Decks: Five.
Normal speed: 20 knots.
Passenger accommodation: 581 in a single first
   class capacity.
Maiden voyage: Le Havre—Fort de France—Pointe à
   Pitre on November 12, 1971.

Built for the Norwegian-America Line and christened *Bergensfjord*. Sold to the French Line in March 1971 to replace their cruise ship Antilles and renamed *De Grasse*. Placed in a Caribbean cruise service out of Pointe à Pitre on February 1, 1972. She sailed out of San Juan every Sunday to La Guaira—Grenada—Martinique—Guadeloupe—St. Croix until April 1973, when she was placed in a cruise service from Le Havre to the Baltic and North Cape with intermediate cruises to the Mediterranean out of Cannes. Equipped with motion stabilisers and fully air-conditioned, the *De Grasse's* superstructure is constructed of aluminum. Sold to the Thorensen Co. of Singapore in mid-1973 and renamed *Rasa Sa Yang*. Presently in their service.

ESPAGNE

Builder: Chantier & Ateliers de Provence, Port de Bouc, France.
Completed: August 1910.
Gross tonnage: 11155.
Dimensions: 545ft × 60ft. Depth 36 ft.
Engines: Two four-cylinder, triple expansion.
Screws: Twin.
Watertight bulkheads: Thirteen.

Decks: Four.
Normal speed: 18 knots. (Attained a speed of 19.48 knots during her trials.)
Passenger accommodation: 296 first, 106 second and 86 third class.
Maiden voyage: St. Nazaire–West Indies on October 5, 1910.

The *Espagne* made several voyages to New York in 1912–19, but was mostly scheduled in the St. Nazaire–Antilles and Mexico service. Sold for scrap at St. Nazaire, France, in April 1934.

FLANDRE

Builder: Ateliers & Chantiers de France, Dunkirk, France.

Completed: 1952.

Gross tonnage: 20477.

Dimensions: 600ft × 80ft. Depth 46ft.

Engines: Eight Rateau double-reduction geared turbines.

Screws: Twin.

Decks: Five.

Normal speed: 23 knots.

Passenger accommodation: 407 first and 621 tourist class.

Maiden voyage: Le Havre—New York on July 23, 1952.

Bulkheads: Nine.

Her maiden voyage was marred while *en route* to New York when electrical faultiness and fuel pump disorders forced her to return to Dunkirk for repairs. Re-entered service on April 17, 1953, after her embarrassing incident the year before. Engaged in the Le Havre—Southampton—New York run, and cruising. Reconditioned in early 1955 and resumed sailings on April 29, 1955. Reallocated to the West Indies trade in 1965 and finally sold to the Coast Lines in December 1967 and renamed *Carla C* in 1968. Presently in their service.

Sister ship: *Antilles.*

II FRANCE

Builder: Chantiers & Ateliers de St. Nazaire, Pehoet, France.
Completed: January 1912.
Gross tonnage: 23769.
Dimensions: 720ft × 76ft. Depth 48ft.
Engines: Four direct-action steam turbines.
Screws: Quadruple.
Watertight bulkheads: Sixteen.
Decks: Five.
Normal speed: 23.50 knots. (Attained a speed of 25.09 knots on her trials.)
Officers and crew: 600.
Passenger accommodation: 535 first, 442 second and 948 third class.
Maiden voyage: Le Havre–New York on April 20, 1912.

She was laid down as *La Picardie*, but changed to *France* upon resumption of work. Employed in the Le Havre–New York run in 1914 she was laid up at the outbreak of World War I and transported troops from March 1915 until May of that year under the name of *France IV*. Laid up and commissioned as a hospital ship in November 1915 until May 1917. In March 1918 she transported American troops until February 1919 and resumed sailings under her original name in August. She was France's first turbine liner and was constructed with a double bottom. Her coal consumption was 720 tons every 24 hours. Overhauled in 1923 and converted to oil firing. She commenced her last voyage for the French Line on August 13, 1932, from Le Havre to Plymouth and New York and was laid up in September. Among the many recreational pastimes on board passenger ships as shuffleboard or trap shooting–to mention a few–the *France* went further by employing a bowling lane on her boat deck. In the course of her life's history the *France* seemed to have a streak of bad luck when it came to fire. In 1912 she had a fire in her coal bunkers while on her trials; in 1919 there was an explosion on board which killed nine men; another at her dock in 1933 and once again in 1935 while she was being dismantled. Sold for scrap in November 1934 and left for the ship-breaker's yard at Dunkirk on April 15, 1935.

III FRANCE

Builder: Chantiers de L'Atlantique, St. Nazaire, France.
Completed: 1961.
Gross tonnage: 66348.
Dimensions: 1035ft × 111ft. Depth 81ft.
Engines: Sixteen steam turbines single-reduction geared.
Screws: Quadruple.
Decks: Seven.
Normal speed: 31 knots. (Attained a speed of 34.13 knots on her trials.)
Passenger accommodation: 500 first, and 1500 tourist class.
Maiden voyage: Le Havre—Southampton—New York on February 3, 1962.
Last voyage: New York—Southampton—Le Havre on September 5, 1974.

Employed in the Le Havre—Southampton—New York service with cruises on occasion to the West Indies. The *France* made a 40-day cruise to the West Indies, South America and South Africa from New York on January 6, 1971. Equipped with motion stabilisers and fully air-conditioned she is the Line's flagship. *France* is the longest ship in the world and with the *Queen Elizabeth* out of service, she is theoretically the largest also. A very handsome ship though her funnels seem quite odd with their ear-like exhausts on the side of each funnel. *(See Notes on p. 223.)*

ILE DE FRANCE

Builder: Chantiers de St. Nazaire, France.
Completed: 1926.
Gross tonnage: 44356.
Dimensions: 793ft × 92ft. Depth 56ft.
Engines: Four direct-acting Parson steam turbines.
Screws: Quadruple.
Watertight bulkheads: Fifteen.
Decks: Six.
Normal speed: 23 knots.
Officers and crew: 700.
Passenger accommodation: 637 cabin and 509 tourist class.
Maiden voyage: Le Havre–Plymouth–New York on June 22, 1927.

The *Ile de France* was the first ship to carry a small seaplane catapult on her boat deck for the dispatching of mail and the first on the North Atlantic to have her lifeboats set on gravity davits. The entrance to her grand vestibule was four decks high and to keep the optimistic investor of the 'twenties well informed, a stock ticker was among her luxuries. Employed in the Le Havre–Plymouth–New York run inaugurating a call at Southampton since January 30, 1935, and calling at Plymouth eastbound only. The *Ile de France* left New York on May 1, 1940, for the Orient after having been converted to a transport and was seized by the British at Singapore on July 19, 1940, and put under the auspices of the British Ministry of Transport with management under the Cunard Line. She was decommissioned on September 22, 1945, and transported displaced persons until April 16, 1947, when she reverted back to her owners. During her career she transported over 300000 troops and plied over 500000 miles. Resumed transatlantic sailings on July 21, 1949, after being almost completely rebuilt over a period of two years. Her outward appearance changed by the elimination of her three stacks by two of different design. On the night of July 26, 1956, the *Ile de France* answered the distress call from the sinking Italian Line ship *Andrea Doria*, after collision with the Swedish-America liner *Stockholm* off the Nantucket Shoals, and rescued over 700 people. Commenced her last voyage for the French Line from New York to Plymouth and Le Havre on November 10, 1958, and was subsequently laid up. Sold to Japanese shipbreakers on January 12, 1959, and sailed from Le Havre to Osaka on February 26 under the name *Furansu Maru*, which means, 'The French Ship'. A courtesy well deserved to a lovely and most popular ship of many, if not all, who came to know her. Her name will always be aside those splendid ships that were said to have possessed a soul. Broken up by September 1959.

II LAFAYETTE

Builder: Chantiers & Ateliers de Provence, Marseilles, France.

Completed: 1915.

Gross tonnage: 12220.

Dimensions: 546ft × 64ft. Depth 35ft.

Engines: Two four-cylinder quadruple expansion engines and two Parson low-pressure steam turbines.

Screws: Quadruple.

Watertight bulkheads: Thirteen.

Decks: Four.

Normal speed: 16.50 knots. (Attained a speed of 18.09 knots on her trial runs.)

Passenger accommodation: 336 first, 110 second and 90 third class.

Maiden voyage: Bordeaux–New York on November 3, 1915.

She was to be named *Ile De Cuba* for the West Indies trade but changed to *Lafayette* after launching. Converted to a hospital ship in 1916 and resumed transatlantic sailings after hostilities ceased in 1918. Engaged in the Le Havre–New York service until 1928 when she was renamed *Mexique* and reallocated to the St. Nazaire–Vera Cruz–West Indies trade for which she was originally designed. Sunk by a mine in the Gironde Estuary, France on June 19, 1940.

III LAFAYETTE

Builder: Chantiers & Ateliers de St. Nazaire, Penhoet, France.
Completed: 1929.
Gross tonnage: 25178.
Dimensions: 613ft × 78ft. Depth 45ft.
Engines: Four MAN, six-cylinder, two-stroke, double-acting diesel.
Screws: Quadruple.
Watertight bulkheads: Seventeen.
Decks: Five.
Normal speed: 17 knots.
Officers and crew: 472.
Passenger accommodation: 591 cabin, 334 tourist and 142 third class.
Maiden voyage: Le Havre—Plymouth—New York on May 17, 1930.
Last voyage: New York—Le Havre on April 20, 1938.

Engaged in the Le Havre—Plymouth—New York run, and cruising. In March 1934 she ran into a gale in the Atlantic and hove to for almost five hours, damaging many windows and upper works. Quite similar to the *Champlain* in appearance though they differed in their propelling machinery. The *Lafayette* was destroyed by fire while in dry dock at Le Havre on May 4, 1938. The remaining hulk was sold to shipbreakers at Rotterdam, Holland. *(See Notes on p. 223.)*

LA LORRAINE

Builder: Compagnie Generale Transatlantique,
St. Nazaire, France.
Completed: 1900.
Gross tonnage: 11372.
Dimensions: 580ft × 60ft. Depth 35ft.
Engines: Two four-cylinder, triple expansion.
Screws: Twin.
Decks: Four.
Normal speed: 20 knots. (Attained a speed of
21.80 knots on her trial runs.)
Officers and crew: 410.
Passenger accommodation: 446 first, 116
second and 552 steerage.
Maiden voyage: Le Havre—New York on
August 11, 1900.
Last voyage: New York—Le Havre on October 14,
1922.

She had 18 boilers and 190 stokers to man the stokeholds. Employed in the Le Havre—New York run year-round. She was mobilised as a transport at the outbreak of World War I in August 1914 and renamed *Lorraine II.* She was later converted to an armed merchant cruiser in April 1917 and resumed regular sailings after the war under her original name. The *Lorraine* and her sister ship *La Savoie* were fast steamers of their day and became well known on the Atlantic Ferry. Sold for scrap at St. Nazaire, France, in December 1922.
Sister ship: *La Savoie.*

LA PROVENCE

Builder: Chantiers & Ateliers de St. Nazaire,
  Penhoet, France.
Completed: 1906.
Gross tonnage: 13753.
Dimensions: 627ft × 65ft. Depth 38ft.
Engines: Two four-cylinder, triple expansion.
Screws: Twin.
Decks: Four.
Normal speed: 21 knots. (Attained a speed of
  23 knots during her trials.)
Passenger accommodation: 358 first class, 339
  second, and 898 third.
Maiden voyage: Le Havre–New York on
  April 21, 1906.
Last commercial voyage: New York–Le Havre on
  June 17, 1914.
Bulkheads: Twenty-one.

Employed in the Le Havre–New York run year-round. In the year 1907 she transported over 107000 immigrants to the port of New York. Converted to an armed merchant cruiser in December 1914 and renamed *Provence II*. Torpedoed and sunk while *en route* from Toulon, France, to Salonica, Greece, with an estimated 1700 troops on board, by U-35 in the Aegean Sea on February 26, 1916. There was a loss of 830 lives.

LA SAVOIE

Builder: Compagnie Generale Transatlantique, St. Nazaire, France.
Completed: 1901.
Gross tonnage: 11168.
Dimensions: 580ft × 60ft. Depth 35ft.
Engines: Two four-cylinder, triple expansion.
Screws: Twin.
Decks: Four.
Normal speed: 20 knots.
Officers and crew: 410.
Passenger accommodation: 437 first, 118 second and 398 steerage.
Maiden voyage: Le Havre–New York on August 31, 1901.

She had 18 boilers and 190 stokers to man the fifty coal bins. Engaged in the Le Havre–New York run year-round. Mobilised as an armed merchant cruiser in August 1914 and renamed *Savoie II*. Placed back in the transatlantic run in 1918 and altered to cabin- and third-class accommodations in 1923. She and her sister *La Lorraine* were presented in the usual plush designs of French decor for which they were both well known and remembered. Sold to shipbreakers at Dunkirk, France, in November 1927.
Sister ship: *La Lorraine.*

LIBERTE

Builder: Blohm & Voss, Hamburg, Germany.
Completed: March 1930.
Gross tonnage: 51839.
Dimensions: 937ft × 102 ft. Depth 48ft.
Engines: Twelve turbines single-reduction geared.
Screws: Quadruple.
Watertight bulkheads: Fourteen.
Decks: Seven.
Normal speed: 24.50 knots.
Passenger accommodation: 555 first, 497 cabin and 450 tourist class.
Maiden voyage: Le Havre–New York on August 17, 1950.

Built for the North German Lloyd and christened *Europa.* Allotted to the French Government in May 1946 as a World War II reparation and transferred to the French Line in July and renamed *Liberte.* The name *Lorraine* had been contemplated, but *Liberte* seemed more appropriate after the war. On December 9, 1946, the *Liberte* had broken loose from her moorings during a severe gale and rammed into the sunken hulk of the *Paris* in the harbour at Le Havre and damaged her starboard side extensively. She was scuttled to prevent her from capsizing. Refloated on April 15, 1947, and taken to St. Nazaire in November and reconstructed at a cost of about $19 million. Engaged in the Le Havre–Channel ports–New York service. New funnels were fitted in 1954 that were of odd shape and height causing her to look greatly out of proportion. Sold to Italian shipbreakers on December 30, 1961, and broken up by June 1962.

NORMANDIE

Builder: Chantiers & Ateliers de St. Nazaire, Penhoet, France.
Completed: 1935.
Gross tonnage: 83423.
Dimensions: 1027ft × 118ft. Depth 58ft.
Engines: Four steam turbines connected to four electric motors.
Screws: Quadruple.
Decks: Ten.
Normal speed: 30 knots. (Attained a speed of 31.95 knots on her trial runs.)
Officers and crew: 1320.
Passenger accommodation: 848 first, 670 tourist and 454 third class.
Maiden voyage: Le Havre—Southampton—New York on May 29, 1935.
Bulkheads: Eleven.
Last voyage: Le Havre—Southampton—New York, arriving on August 28, 1939.

She won the Blue Riband from the Italian Line's *Rex* on her maiden voyage by making the run from Bishop Rock to Ambrose Lighthouse in 4 days, 3 hours and 14 minutes at a speed of 29.94 knots. The *Normandie*'s main dining room was three decks high and 270ft long with a seating capacity of 1000. Built with a bulbous bow to increase her speed. Her funnels were 160ft in circumference and 145ft in height. Her swimming pool was 100ft long and 30ft wide. In March 1936 her superstructure was enlarged to give her the present tonnage and acclaiming to be the largest ship in the world. Each of her propellers weighs 23 tons and measure 15ft in diameter. Employed in the Le Havre—Southampton—New York run until she was laid up at New York on August 28, 1939, and seized by the United States on December 16, 1941,

for conversion to a transport with renaming to *Lafayette*. Caught fire by a worker's acetylene torch that ignited some bedding which had been brought on board prematurely whilst fitting out on February 9, 1942. As the fire raged on, the water was poured in by the ton from fireboats and from the docks and when she became top heavy because of the great intake of water she keeled over on her port side at the French Line's quay in 50ft of water. Refloated by the Americans on August 9, 1943, at a cost of $4 million. Anticipating further costs for reconstruction she was sold to Lipsett Incorporated for $161680 and was scrapped at Port Newark, New Jersey in September 1946. It was a pity she lived such a short life for she was the pride of France at the time of building and was lost in the hands of strangers.

PARIS

Builder: Chantiers & Ateliers de St. Nazaire,
  Penhoet, France.
Completed: 1921.
Gross tonnage: 34569.
Dimensions: 763ft × 85ft. Depth 59ft.
Engines: Four direct-action Parson steam
  turbines.
Screws: Quadruple.
Watertight bulkheads: Fourteen.
Decks: Five.
Normal speed: 22 knots. (Attained a speed of
  22.44 knots on her trials.)
Officers and crew: 664.
Passenger accommodation: 340 first, 163
  tourist and 409 third class.
Maiden voyage: Le Havre—New York on
  June 15, 1921.
Last voyage: New York—Le Havre on April 8, 1939.

Actually launched on September 12, 1916. Construction was held up during World War I and the hull was towed to Quiberon, France where it remained until brought back to St. Nazaire in 1921 and completed. Employed in the Le Havre—Channel ports—New York service. Her passenger accommodations were burnt out at Le Havre in August 1929 and she did not resume sailings until January 1930. The *Paris* had a promenade deck that extended 423ft in length and her grand dining room could accommodate 540 persons each sitting. On April 18, 1939, the *Paris* was again consumed in flames. This time it was fatal and she keeled over and sank in the harbour at Le Havre the next day. Her hulk remained in the harbour for many years and was not removed until after the Line's *Liberte* broke from her moorings on the night of December 9, 1946, and rammed into the wreck. The largest merchant ship of France when built, she was a favourite of the many who sailed in her and was a fine example of French ship-building.

ROCHAMBEAU

Builder: Chantiers de L'Atlantique de St. Nazaire, Penhoet, France.
Completed: August 1911.
Gross tonnage: 12678.
Dimensions: 559ft × 64ft. Depth 43ft.
Engines: Two four-cylinder triple expansion engines and two BP turbines.
Screws: Quadruple.
Watertight bulkheads: Thirteen.
Decks: Four.
Normal speed: 15.50 knots. (Attaining a speed of 17.50 knots on her trial runs.)
Passenger accommodation: 628 in second and third class and 1248 steerage.
Maiden voyage: Le Havre—New York on November 16, 1911.

Employed in the Le Havre—Channel ports—New York run and was reallocated to the Bordeaux—New York service in 1915 until 1918. She repatriated American troops in 1919 and was demobilised in 1920. Proceeded on her last voyage for the French Line from Le Havre to Plymouth and New York on August 3, 1932, and was subsequently laid up on her return voyage. Sold for scrap to Gosselin & Dumouries at Dunkirk, France, in May 1934.

SUFFREN

Builder: Blohm & Voss, Hamburg, Germany.
Completed: November 1901.
Gross tonnage: 11948.
Dimensions: 527ft × 62ft. Depth 36ft.
Engines: Two four-cylinder quadruple expansion.
Screws: Twin.
Decks: Four.
Normal speed: 15 knots.
Passenger accommodation: 500 second and 250 third class.
Maiden voyage: Le Havre–New York on May 8, 1923.

Built for the Hamburg-America Line and christened *Bluecher*. Seized by the Brazilian Government at Recife on October 26, 1917, and renamed *Leopoldina*. Chartered to the French Line in 1920 and purchased by them in 1923 with renaming to *Suffren*. Employed in the Le Havre–New York run but was reallocated to make her initial sailings from Bordeaux. Made her last voyage for the Line on December 22, 1928, and was sold for scrap in Genoa, Italy, in May 1929.

II VILLE D'ALGER

Builder: Chantiers & Ateliers de St. Nazaire, Penhoet, France.
Completed: 1935.
Gross tonnage: 10172.
Dimensions: 492ft × 63ft. Depth 35ft.
Engines: Six steam turbines single-reduction geared.
Screws: Twin.
Decks: Three.
Normal speed: 21 knots.
Passenger accommodation: 156 first, 422 tourist and 950 fourth class.
Maiden voyage: Marseilles–Algiers on September 2, 1935.
Watertight bulkheads: Seven.

Engaged in the Marseilles–Algiers–North African ports trade. Requisitioned for troop service during World War II and scuttled by the Germans at Port de Bouc, France, in August 1944. Refloated and reconstructed after the war with the elimination of her former two funnels by a new single one of modern design and a reduction in tonnage to 9890 gross tons. Re-entered service on her regular route in 1948. Sold to the Typaldos Lines in 1966 and renamed *Poseidon.* Sold for scrap at Spezia, Italy, where breaking-up commenced on June 20, 1969.
Sister ship: *Ville D'Oran.*

VILLE D'ORAN

Builder: Societe Provencale de Constructions
  Navales, La Ciotat, France.
Completed: 1936.
Gross tonnage: 10172.
Dimensions: 492ft × 63ft. Depth 35ft.
Engines: Six Parson steam turbines single-
  reduction geared.
Screws: Twin.
Decks: Three.
Normal speed: 24 knots.
Passenger accommodation: 149 first, 334
  tourist and 671 fourth class.
Maiden voyage: Marseilles–Oran on October 17,
  1936.
Watertight bulkheads: Seven.

Employed in the Marseilles–Oran–North African
ports trade. Requisitioned by the British Ministry of
Transport during World War II and managed by the
Cunard Line. Decommissioned in June 1946 and
reconstructed with her two funnels replaced by
a single one of modern design. Re-entered service
in 1954. The *Ville D'Oran* was the fastest ship engaged in the Mediterranean. Sold to the Typaldos
Lines in June 1965 and renamed *Mount Olympos*.
Sold for scrap at Trieste, Italy, where breaking up
commenced on July 1, 1970.
Sister ship: *Ville D'Alger.*

The French Line's flagship *France* leaving New York with the *Ocean Monarch* in the background.

GREEK LINE

ARKADIA

Builder: Vickers, Armstrong Ltd, Newcastle-on-Tyne, England.
Completed: November 1931.
Gross tonnage: 20648.
Dimensions: 590ft × 84ft. Depth 43ft.
Engines: Two steam turbines connected to four electric motors.
Screws: Quadruple.
Collision bulkheads: One.
Watertight bulkheads: Eleven.
Decks: Five.
Normal speed: 19.50 knots.
Passenger accommodation: 55 first and 1331 tourist class.
Maiden voyage: Bremerhaven–Southampton–Liverpool–Greenock–Quebec–Montreal on May 22, 1958.

Built for the Furness-Bermuda Line and christened *Monarch of Bermuda*. Sold to Shaw, Savill & Albion Co in 1949 and renamed *New Australia*. Resold to the Greek Line in December 1957 and renamed *Arkadia*. Employed in the Bremerhaven–Amsterdam–London–Le Havre–Cobh–Quebec–Montreal service with cruises out of Southampton to the Baltic seaports during the summer months. She was later employed for year-round cruising in the early months of 1966 to ports of her usual cruise service and to the Canary islands. Laid up in the summer of 1966 in the Fal River, England, until sold to the Desguaces Maritimos in December and broken up in January 1967 at Castellon, Spain.
Note: The *Arkadia* originally had three funnels and a straight stem when built as the *Monarch of Bermuda*. She was reconstructed prior to her sale to the Greek Line.

LAKONIA

Builder: Nederlandsche Scheepsbouw, Maats, Amsterdam, Netherlands.
Completed: 1930.
Gross tonnage: 20314.
Dimensions: 609ft × 75ft. Depth 36ft.
Engines: Two ten-cylinder, two-stroke, single-acting diesel engines.
Screws: Twin.
Decks: Five.
Normal speed: 17 knots.
Officers and crew: 335.
Passenger accommodation: 693 in a single first-class capacity.
Maiden voyage: Southampton—Madeira—Tenerife—Las Palmas—Tangier—Lisbon—Le Havre—Southampton on April 24, 1963, in the form of a cruise.

Built for the Nederland Royal Mail Line and christened *Johan Van Oldenbarnevelt*. Sold to the Greek Line in early 1963, renamed *Lakonia*. Engaged in the Southampton—Canary Islands—Iberian ports—Le Havre—Southampton cruise service. On December 22, 1963 while on her eighteenth voyage out the *Lakonia* caught fire *en route* to Madeira. She was taken in tow, but keeled over 250 miles west of Gibraltar. At the Greek inquiry it was brought to light that no boat drill had been executed on the following day out of Southampton and an ill-trained crew had been employed to run the ship. The crew's inexperience in fire-fighting caused 132 people to lose their lives of the 1028 on board. The loss of this newly acquired vessel had been a severe breach to the Line's services and the cancellation of 26 cruises which had been scheduled for the following year by the *Lakonia*.

NEPTUNIA

Builder: Nederlandsche Scheepsbouw, Maats,. Amsterdam, Netherlands.
Completed: February 1920.
Gross tonnage: 10519.
Dimensions: 523ft × 59ft. Depth 38ft.
Engines: Two three-cylinder triple expansion.
Screws: Twin.
Watertight bulkheads: Ten.
Decks: Three.
Normal speed: 16 knots.
Passenger accommodation: 39 first and 748 tourist class.
Maiden voyage: Piraeus–Genoa–New York in 1949.

Built for the Nederland Royal Mail Line and christened *Johan De Witt*. Sold to the Greek Line in 1948 and renamed *Neptunia*. Engaged in the Piraeus–Mediterranean ports–New York run. Re-allocated to the Bremerhaven–Southampton–Cherbourg–Halifax–New York run on March 30, 1951. Diverted once again to a new route on April 15, 1955, from Bremerhaven to Southampton, Cherbourg and Montreal, this was now a regular service from Bremerhaven to Southampton, Cherbourg, Cobh, Quebec and Montreal in summer and to New York via these ports in winter with a call at Boston on occasion eastbound. The *Neptunia* met with the misfortune of striking Daunt's Rock just outside of Cobh, Ireland, on November 2, 1957, while *en route* to Bremerhaven and was beached on Whitegate Roads seriously damaged. Sold to Dutch shipbreakers and arrived in tow at the New Waterway, Netherlands on March 7, 1958.

Note: The *Neptunia* originally had two funnels when constructed in 1920, but was reconstructed with one prior to her purchase by the Greek Line.

NEW YORK

Builder: Fairfield Shipbuilding & Engineering Co
Ltd, Glasgow, Scotland.
Completed: September 1922.
Gross tonnage: 16991.
Dimensions: 579ft × 70ft. Depth 39ft.
Engines: Six steam turbines, double-reduction
geared.
Screws: Twin.
Watertight bulkheads: Ten.
Decks: Four.
Normal speed: 16 knots.
Passenger accommodation: 73 first and 1173
tourist class.
Maiden voyage: Piraeus–New York in 1939.

Built for the Anchor Line and christened *Tuscania*.
Sold to the Greek Line in April 1939 and renamed
Nea Hellas; 'New York' in March 1955. Engaged in
the Piraeus–Valetta–Naples–Lisbon–Halifax–New
York run westbound and calling at Lisbon, Naples
and Piraeus eastbound with an occasional call at
Boston or Ponta Delgarda homeward. Requisitioned by the British Ministry of Transport in 1941
and managed by her former owners, the Anchor
Line, throughout the war years in which course
she acquired the nickname of 'Nellie Wallace' as
she was known by the British troops. Re-entered
service in 1947 after having been overhauled. Re-

allocated to the New York–Cobh–Southampton–
Bremerhaven run on March 24, 1955, extending
to September 17, 1959, when she reverted back to
the Mediterranean route. On October 13, 1959,
she made a round trip to Quebec from Piraeus via
Naples and was later placed in a cruise service out
of Southampton to Madeira and the Canary
Islands. Withdrawn in late 1960. Sold to shipbreakers at Onomichi, Japan and left Piraeus for
the last time on August 19, 1961, arriving at the
shipbreaker's yards in October and subsequently
broken up.

OLYMPIA

Builder: Alexander Stephen & Sons Ltd, Glasgow, Scotland.

Completed: October 1953.

Gross tonnage: 17434.

Dimensions: 611ft × 79ft. Depth 47ft.

Engines: Four steam turbines double-reduction geared.

Screws: Twin.

Collision bulkhead: One.

Watertight bulkheads: Ten.

Decks: Five.

Normal speed: 21 knots.

Passenger accommodation: 138 first and 1169 tourist class. (Accommodations are restricted to 650 when pleasure-cruising.)

Maiden voyage: Glasgow–Belfast–Liverpool–Southampton–Cherbourg–Cobh–Halifax–New York on October 15, 1953.

Officers and crew: 350.

Last voyage: New York–Naples–Messina–Haifa–Piraeus on March 11, 1974.

Employed in the Bremerhaven–Southampton–Cherbourg–Cobh–New York run until March 26, 1955, when she was placed in the New York–Mediterranean ports–Piraeus service. The *Olympia*'s itinerary now was confined to the Mediterranean almost year-round with some cruising to the West Indies out of New York during the colder months. By 1961 her route was Haifa–Piraeus–Messina–Naples–Lisbon–Halifax–New York outward and New York–Lisbon–Naples–Messina–

Piraeus–Limassol–Haifa with an occasional call at Boston homeward. Placed in a weekly service to Bermuda, and to the West Indies periodically working out of New York since 1969. She was overhauled in 1970 and her passenger accommodation remodelled for cruise services. In 1971 underwent a major refit costing over four million dollars to be converted from a two-class ship to a one-class luxury cruise ship. She now accommodates 1030 persons. *(See Notes on p. 223.)*

QUEEN ANNA MARIA

Builder: Fairfield Shipbuilding & Engineering
Co Ltd, Glasgow, Scotland.
Completed: March 1956.
Gross tonnage: 21716.
Dimensions: 640ft × 85ft. Depth 48ft.
Engines: Six steam turbines, double-reduction
geared.
Screws: Twin.
Collision bulkhead: One.
Watertight bulkheads: Ten.
Decks: Five.
Normal speed: 21 knots.
Passenger accommodation: 109 first and
1145 tourist class.
Maiden voyage: Piraeus–Palermo–Naples–
Lisbon–Halifax–New York in 1965.
Last commercial voyage: New York–Boston–Ponta
Delgada–Lisbon–Valetta–Piraeus–Haifa on No-
vember 12, 1974.

Built for the Canadian-Pacific Lines and christ-
ened *Empress of Britain*. Sold to the Greek Line in
1964 and renamed *Queen Anna Maria*. She is the
Greek Line's flagship and is engaged in the Haifa–
Piraeus–Messina–Naples–New York run west-
bound calling at Lisbon, Piraeus, Limassol and
Haifa westbound and sometimes calls at Boston,
Azores, and Valetta eastbound. The *Queen Anna
Maria* cruises in conjunction with her running
mate *Olympia* to the West Indies a few voyages
each year when the latter goes to dry-docking in
Piraeus annually. Equipped with motion stabi-
lisers and fully air-conditioned.
(See Notes on p. 223.)

HOLLAND-AMERICA LINE

IV MAASDAM

Builder: N.V. Wilton, Fijenoord, Schiedam, Netherlands.
Completed: July 1952.
Gross tonnage: 15024.
Dimensions: 503ft × 69ft. Depth 42ft.
Engines: Two steam turbines, double-reduction geared.
Screws: Single.
Watertight bulkheads: Eight.
Decks: Four.
Normal speed: 16.50 knots.
Passenger accommodation: 39 first and 836 tourist class.
Maiden voyage: Rotterdam—New York on August 11, 1952.

Engaged in the Rotterdam—Cobh—New York run until 1963 when she was stationed at Bremerhaven making Rotterdam her first port of call then proceeding to other ports in the Channel and on to New York with cruising during the off season. On October 18, 1965, she made a voyage from Bremerhaven to Rotterdam and Southampton via Suez Canal, Fremantle, Melbourne, Sydney and Wellington. Sold to the Polish Ocean Lines in December 1968 and renamed *Stefan Batory* in 1969. Presently in their service.
Sister ship: *Ryndam*

I NIEUW AMSTERDAM

Builder: Harland & Wolff Ltd, Belfast, Ireland.
Completed: February 1906.
Gross tonnage: 17149.
Dimensions: 616ft × 69ft. Depth 36ft.
Engines: Two four-cylinder, quadruple expansion.
Screws: Twin.
Watertight bulkheads: Ten.
Decks: Four.
Normal speed: 16 knots.
Passenger accommodation: 417 first, 391 second and 2300 steerage.
Maiden voyage: Rotterdam–New York on April 7, 1906.

Engaged in the Rotterdam–New York run and continued regular sailings throughout World War I. By 1923 her itinerary included a call at Boulogne and Southampton westbound and Plymouth–Boulogne eastbound. Commenced her last voyage for the Holland-America Line on March 11, 1932, from Rotterdam to Boulogne, Southampton and New York. Sold to Japanese shipbreakers in April 1932.

II NIEUW AMSTERDAM

Builder: Rotterdamsche Droogdok Maats, Co,
  Rotterdam, Netherlands.
Completed: May 1938.
Gross tonnage: 36982.
Dimensions: 759ft × 88ft. Depth 55ft.
Engines: Eight steam turbines single-reduction
  geared.
Screws: Twin.
Collision bulkhead: One.
Watertight bulkheads: Ten.
Decks: Seven.
Normal speed: 21.50 knots.
Passenger accommodation: 691 first and 972
  tourist class.
Maiden voyage: Rotterdam–Boulogne–
  Southampton–New York on May 10, 1938.

Laid down as the *Prinsendam* but changed to *Nieuw Amsterdam* before work commenced. Engaged in the Rotterdam–Southampton–Cobh–New York service. She was sent pleasure cruising in 1938 from New York to the West Indies and laid up at New York in 1939. Taken over by the British Ministry of Transport and refitted at Halifax in September 1940 as a troopship with accommodation for 8000 troops and put under Cunard Line management. Returned to Rotterdam on April 26, 1946, after having steamed over 530000 miles and carrying some 350000 men. Reconditioned after eighteen months and re-entered service on October 29, 1947, from Rotterdam to New York. At the time of her construction she was the largest twin-screw vessel and the largest in the Dutch Mercantile Marine. She has a promenade deck 608ft long and an upper promenade deck of 337ft in length. Built at an estimated cost of £5 million. The *Nieuw Amsterdam* is one of the last vessels on the North Atlantic ferry with old world tastes in design. Engaged in the Rotterdam–Le Havre–Southampton–Cobh–New York service since the late 'fifties and cruising during the off seasons. Withdrawn from North Atlantic service in December 1971 and placed in permanent cruise services. Presently in service.

I NOORDAM

Builder: Harland & Wolff Ltd, Belfast, Ireland.
Completed: March 1902.
Gross tonnage: 12528.
Dimensions: 565ft × 62ft. Depth 34ft.
Engines: Two three-cylinder, triple expansion.
Screws: Twin.
Watertight bulkheads: Ten.
Decks: Four.
Normal speed: 15 knots.
Passenger accommodation: 286 first, 192 second and 1800 third class.
Maiden voyage: Rotterdam–New York on May 1, 1902.

Engaged in the Rotterdam–Channel ports–New York service year-round. Laid up after being damaged twice by mines in the North Sea in 1917. Returned to normal service in March 1919 sailing from Rotterdam to Brest, Falmouth and New York. Chartered to the Swedish-American Line from March 1922 until December 1924 and sailed under the name of *Kungsholm*. Returned to the Line in 1924 and recovered her own name. She was now working on the Rotterdam–Boulogne–Southampton–New York route with a call at Plymouth and Boulogne homeward. Sold to Mr Frank Rijsdijk's Ind. Onderne Mingen in 1927 and scrapped in 1928 in the Netherlands.
Sister ships: *Potsdam* and *Rijndam*.

II NOORDAM

Builder: Maschinefabriek en Scheepswerf van P. Smit Jr, Rotterdam, Netherlands.
Completed: September 1938.
Gross tonnage: 10726.
Dimensions: 502ft × 64ft. Depth 40ft.
Engines: Two 12-cylinder, two-stroke, single-acting diesel.
Screws: Twin.
Watertight bulkheads: Eight.
Decks: Three.
Normal speed: 17 knots.
Passenger accommodation: 123 first-class passengers. She is classified as a cargo-passenger liner.
Maiden voyage: Rotterdam–New York on September 28, 1938.
Last voyage for Holland-America Line: New York –Rotterdam on August 27, 1963.

Engaged in the Rotterdam–Channel ports–New York service until transferred to the Java–East Indies trade in the spring of 1940 and fitted out as a transport in early 1942. Resumed transatlantic service in July 1946 and was sold to the Cielomar Panama in 1963 with renaming to *Oceanien*. Chartered to the Messageries Maritimes for a time. *(See Notes on p. 223.)*
Sister ship: *Zaandam.*

POTSDAM

Builder: Blohm & Voss, Hamburg, Germany.
Completed: May 1900.
Gross tonnage: 12522.
Dimensions: 571ft × 62ft. Depth 38ft.
Engines: Two three-cylinder, triple expansion.
Screws: Twin.
Watertight bulkheads: Ten.
Decks: Four.
Normal speed: 15 knots.
Officers and crew: 248.
Passenger accommodation: 280 first, 220 second and 1700 third class.
Maiden voyage: Rotterdam–New York on May 17, 1900.

Engaged in the Rotterdam–Channel ports–New York service. Her funnel was later heightened because her exhaust did not clear properly, earning her the nickname of 'Funneldam'. The *Potsdam* had a promenade deck 195ft long. Sold to the Swedish–American Line in 1915 and renamed *Stockholm*. Resold to Norwegian Odd Co, AS and converted to a whale factory ship and re-named *Solgimt* in 1928. Captured by the German raider *Pinguin* in the Antarctic and taken to occupied France during World War II. Scuttled by the Germans at Cherbourg, France, in June 1944 after she had been used by them as a tanker. Unable to refloat her after the war she was blown up on August 30, 1946.
Sister ships: *Noordam* and *Rijndam*.

RIJNDAM

Builder: Harland & Wolff Ltd, Belfast, Ireland.
Completed: October 1901.
Gross tonnage: 12535.
Dimensions: 565ft × 62ft. Depth 42ft.
Engines: Two three-cylinder, triple expansion.
Screws: Twin.
Watertight bulkheads: Ten.
Decks: Four.
Normal speed: 15 knots.
Passenger accommodation: 286 first, 192 second and 1500 steerage.
Maiden voyage: Rotterdam–New York on October 10, 1901.

Engaged in the Rotterdam–New York service until 1917 when she was laid up after being damaged by a mine in the North Sea. Taken over by the United States in 1918 while she lay at the port of New York and utilised as a transport. Returned to the Holland-America Line in the autumn of 1919.

In 1923 her itinerary was Rotterdam–Boulogne–Southampton–New York with a call at Plymouth and Boulogne homeward. Sold to Dutch shipbreakers in January 1929.
Sister ships: *Noordam* and *Potsdam*.

IV ROTTERDAM

Builder: Harland & Wolff Ltd, Belfast, Ireland.
Completed: June 1908.
Gross tonnage: 24149.
Dimensions: 668ft × 77ft. Depth 47ft.
Engines: Two four-cylinder, quadruple expansion.
Screws: Twin.
Watertight bulkheads: Twelve.
Decks: Five.
Normal speed: 17 knots.
Passenger accommodation: 539 first and 643 tourist class.
Maiden voyage: Rotterdam–New York on June 13, 1908.
Last voyage: Rotterdam–New York in May 1939.

Employed in the Rotterdam–Channel ports–New York service until she was laid up during the period from 1916 to 1919. Resumed scheduled sailings to New York in February 1919. Converted to oil-firing in 1923 and was settled in the Rotterdam–Boulogne–Southampton–New York run with a call at Plymouth instead of Southampton eastbound. On September 30, 1935, she ran aground on Morant Cays in the West Indies during a severe gale while on a cruise with 424 persons on board. The passengers were taken off the following day by a British steamer and landed where they could make new passage arrangements. The *Rotterdam* was one of the first large Atlantic liners along with the smaller *Nieuw Amsterdam* to be built with a glassed-in promenade deck and was one of the finest ships of her day, both in appearance and profits. *Rotterdam* was a fine example of an Edwardian-class luxury liner and cruise ship with her moderate tempo in speed and plush interiors. *(See Notes on p. 223.)*

V ROTTERDAM

Builder: Rotterdamsche Droogdok Maats,
Rotterdam, Netherlands.
Completed: August 1959.
Gross tonnage: 37783.
Dimensions: 749ft × 94ft. Depth 55ft.
Engines: Six steam turbines double-reduction
geared.
Screws: Twin.
Normal speed: 21 knots.
Officers and crew: 762.
Passenger accommodation: 647 first and 809
tourist class. (Accommodations are limited to
730 when in cruise services.)
Maiden voyage: Rotterdam–Le Havre–
Southampton–Cobh–New York service and
cruising.

In 1966 she was sent on a series of cruises from New York to the Pacific, Mediterranean and the West Indies and making a world cruise every year. On January 22, 1970, she left New York on an 85-day world cruise calling at 22 ports and 16 countries. Equipped with motion stabilisers and fully air-conditioned. *Rotterdam* is the Holland-America Line's flagship and was built at a cost of £13 million. Her theatre has a seating capacity for 607 persons and is the largest on any passenger ship. Engaged in a cruise service from New York to Bermuda, Nassau and the Bahamas, the West Indies and special cruises. The *Rotterdam* makes an annual transatlantic voyage when she goes to Rotterdam for dry docking. She is the largest ship ever built in the Netherlands. Presently in service.

RYNDAM

Builder: N.V. Wilton, Fijenoord, Schiedam, Netherlands,

Completed: July 1951.

Gross tonnage: 15051.

Dimensions: 503ft × 69ft. Depth 42ft.

Engines: Two steam turbines, double-reduction geared.

Screws: Single.

Watertight bulkheads: Eight.

Decks: Four.

Normal speed: 16.50 knots.

Passenger accommodation: 39 first and 842 tourist class.

Maiden voyage: Rotterdam–Le Havre–Southampton–New York on July 16, 1951.

She was originally laid down as the *Dinteldyk*, a freighter, but the plans were altered while still on the stocks. Employed in the Rotterdam–Channel ports–New York service and later placed in the Montreal service with cruises during the winter months. Reallocated to the Rotterdam–Southampton–via Suez Canal–Fremantle–Melbourne–Sydney–Wellington run on November 6, 1964, until February 7, 1966, when she made her last such voyage. Transferred to the Europe-Canada Line on September 14, 1966 and was renamed *Waterman* in 1968 while under charter, but acquired her own name in the same year. Chartered to the Chapman College in Orange, California in 1969 and returned to the Line in May 1970. Re-chartered to the Foreign Study League of Salt Lake City, Utah for two trips from Boston to Cherbourg and Southampton on June 1 and June 20, 1970. Made her last voyage in May 1971 and laid up at Rotterdam after plans for sale to Sovereign Cruises did not materialise.

Sister ship: *Maasdam.*

I STATENDAM

Builder: Harland & Wolff Ltd, Belfast, Ireland.
Completed: August 1898.
Gross tonnage: 10,491.
Dimensions: 530ft × 60ft. Depth 43ft.
Engines: Two three-cylinder, triple expansion.
Screws: Twin.
Watertight bulkheads: Nine.
Decks: Three.
Normal speed: 14.50 knots.
Maiden voyage: Rotterdam–New York in
    August 1898.

The *Statendam*'s promenade deck was 190 ft in
length. Engaged in the Rotterdam–New York run
until sold to the Allan Line in 1911 and renamed
Scotian. Resold to the Canadian-Pacific Line in
1916 and renamed *Marglen* in 1922. Sold to
Italian shipbreakers in 1927.

III STATENDAM

Builder: Harland & Wolff Ltd, Belfast, Ireland.
Completed: April 1929.
Gross tonnage: 28291.
Dimensions: 698ft × 81ft. Depth 54ft.
Engines: Six steam turbines, single-reduction geared.
Screws: Twin.
Collision bulkhead: One.
Watertight bulkheads: Ten.
Decks: Six.
Normal speed: 19 knots.
Officers and crew: 600.
Passenger accommodation: 453 first, 793 tourist and 418 third class.
Maiden voyage: Rotterdam–Boulogne–Southampton–New York on April 11, 1929.

She was launched on September 11, 1924. Construction was held up and she was towed to Rotterdam on April 13, 1927 where she was completed by the Wilton Slipway & Engineering Co. She was built to replace the second ship of this name which was taken over by the British during World War I and renamed *Justicia*, a transport. Engaged in the Rotterdam–Boulogne–Southampton–New York run with a call at Plymouth in place of Southampton eastbound. A very economical and popular ship she was known as the 'Queen of the Spotless Fleet'. Her aft funnel was a dummy. In 1931 she became a two-class ship. Laid up at Rotterdam in September 1939. The *Statendam* was destroyed by crossfire from both sides of the river while engaging the Nazi invaders on May 11, 1940, and remained ablaze for five days, becoming a total loss.

IV STATENDAM

Builder: N.V. Wilton, Fijenoord, Schiedam, Netherlands.
Completed: February 1957.
Gross tonnage: 24294.
Dimensions: 643ft × 81ft. Depth 52ft.
Engines: Four Pametrada steam turbines.
Screws: Twin.
Collision bulkhead: One.

Watertight bulkheads: Ten.
Decks: Five.
Normal speed: 19 knots.
Officers and crew: 437.
Passenger accommodation: 84 first and 868 tourist class.
Maiden voyage: Rotterdam—Le Havre—Southampton—New York on February 6, 1957.

Employed in the Rotterdam—Channel ports—New York run with cruises during the off season. Fully air-conditioned and equipped with motion stabilisers. She has been in a cruise service since 1966 from Los Angeles and New York to the Pacific, the Mediterranean, the Baltic Sea and the West Indies. Presently in service.

II VEENDAM

Builder: Harland & Wolff Ltd, Glasgow, Scotland.
Completed: March 1923.
Gross tonnage: 15652.
Dimensions: 576ft × 67ft. Depth 45ft.
Engines: Four steam turbines, single-reduction geared.
Screws: Twin.
Watertight bulkheads: Nine.
Decks: Five
Normal speed: 15 knots.
Passenger accommodation: 223 first and 363 tourist class.
Maiden voyage: Rotterdam–Boulogne–Plymouth–New York on April 18, 1923.

Engaged in the Rotterdam–Boulogne–Southampton–New York service with a call at Plymouth in place of Southampton eastbound. In September 1939 she rescued survivors from the sinking British aircraft carrier *Courageous*. Seized by the Germans in May 1940 and used for a submarine depot ship in the Baltic Sea. Sunk at Hamburg on August 2, 1945, and refloated on October 25, 1945. Taken in tow to Ymuiden, Holland, where she arrived on January 16, 1946, for temporary repairs. Left Ymuiden on January 31, 1947, for Rotterdam to be rebuilt and placed back in service in early 1947. Commenced her last voyage for the Holland-America Line on October 30, 1953, from Rotterdam to New York and was sold for scrap to the Bethlehem Steel Corporation at Baltimore, Maryland, in the United States in the same year.
Sister ship: *Volendam*.

VOLENDAM

Builder: Harland & Wolff Ltd, Glasgow, Scotland.
Completed: October 1922.
Gross tonnage: 15434.
Dimensions: 576ft × 67ft. Depth 45ft.
Engines: Four steam turbines, single-reduction geared.
Screws: Twin.
Watertight bulkheads: Nine.
Decks: Five.
Normal speed: 15 knots.
Passenger accommodation: 250 first and 335 tourist class.
Maiden voyage: Rotterdam–Boulogne–Plymouth–New York on November 4, 1922.

Engaged in the Rotterdam–Boulogne–Southampton–New York run with a call at Plymouth eastbound in place of Southampton. The *Volendam* chanced to be at sea when the Germans invaded the Netherlands on May 10, 1940, and from then on worked out of British ports. Torpedoed by a submarine 200 miles north-west of Bloody Foreland, Ireland, on August 30, 1940, while in a westbound convoy and was beached on the island of Bute. The stricken ship's passengers were transferred to assisting vessels and the liner was brought back to the Clyde for repairs and emerged as a transport ten months later under the control of the British Ministry of Transport and under Cunard Line management. Reconditioned after the war to some extent and chartered by the Dutch Government for a period carrying passengers in a single class. Made her last North Atlantic crossing in November 1951 from New York to Rotterdam and was sold for scrap in the Netherlands in January 1952.
Sister ship: *Veendam.*

WESTERDAM

Builder: N.V. Wilton-Fijenoord, Schiedam, Netherlands.
Completed: June 1946.
Gross tonnage: 12149.
Dimensions: 518ft × 66ft. Depth 41ft.
Engines: Two five-cylinder, two-stroke, double-acting diesel.
Screws: Twin.
Decks: Three.
Normal speed: 16 knots.
Passenger accommodation: 152 first-class passengers.
Maiden voyage: Rotterdam–New York on June 30, 1946.

She was launched in 1940 but scuttled three times by the Dutch underground to prevent usage by the German invaders. Refloated after the war and completed in June 1946. Employed in the Rotterdam–Channel ports–New York service. The *Westerdam* is classified as a cargo-passenger liner and was the first post-war passenger ship to sail for America by the Holland-America Line when she arrived in New York on July 8, 1946. Withdrawn from service in December 1964 and sold to Spanish shipbreakers. *(See Notes on p. 223.)*
Sister ship: *Zuiderdam.*

II ZAANDAM

Builder: N.V. Wilton-Fijenoord, Schiedam, Netherlands.
Completed: January 1939.
Gross tonnage: 10909.
Dimensions: 502ft × 64ft. Depth 40ft.
Engines: Two six-cylinder, two-stroke, double-acting diesel.
Screws: Twin.
Watertight bulkheads: Eight.
Decks: Three.
Normal speed: 16.50 knots.
Passenger accommodation: 140 first-class passengers.
Maiden voyage: Rotterdam–New York on January 7, 1939.

Engaged in the Rotterdam–New York service. Transferred to the New York–Java–East Indies trade in the spring of 1940 and fitted out as a transport in early 1942. Sunk by a submarine 400 miles off Cape Recife, Brazil, on November 7, 1942, while *en route* from Beira to New York. There was a loss of 124 people who were never accounted for of her 299 passengers and crew. 82 days later, three survivors were picked up by a United States Navy patrol ship. To this day it is the longest period that anybody has ever been known to endure the open sea.
Sister ship: *Noordam.*

The Nieuw Amsterdam slowly steaming out of the harbour for the open sea.

ARGENTINA

Builder: Cammell, Laird & Co Ltd, Birkenhead,
  England.
Completed: September 1913.
Gross tonnage: 11015.
Dimensions: 530ft × 61ft. Depth 33ft.
Engines: Two four-cylinder, quadruple-expansion
  engines and two low-pressure turbines. double-
  reduction geared.
Screws: Twin.
Watertight bulkheads: Eight.
Desks: Three.
Normal speed: 15 knots.
Passenger accommodation: 32 first and 969
  tourist class.
Maiden voyage: Genoa–Rio de Janeiro–
  Buenos Aires on January 13, 1947.

Built for the Norwegian-America Line and
christened *Bergensfjord*. Sold to the Home Lines
in November 1946 and renamed *Argentina*.
Engaged in the South American trade until
September 1949 when her route was limited to
the Genoa–Central American trade. Reallocated
once again in the spring of 1952 to the Genoa–
Naples–New York service. Sold to the Zim Lines
in the spring of 1953 and renamed *Jerusalem*.
Aliya in 1957. Laid up in May 1958 and sold to
the Terrestse Marittima for scrapping at Spezia,
Italy in October 1959.

ATLANTIC

Builder: William Cramp & Sons Shipbuilding &
Engineering Co, Philadelphia, Pennsylvania,
USA.
Completed: October 1927.
Gross tonnage: 21239.
Dimensions: 582ft × 83ft. Depth 45ft.
Engines: Eight steam turbines single-reduction
geared.
Screws: Twin.
Watertight bulkheads: Twelve.
Decks: Five.
Normal speed: 22 knots.
Passenger accommodation: 349 first, 203
cabin and 626 tourist class.
Maiden voyage: Genoa–New York on May 14,
1949.

Built for the Matson Lines and christened *Malolo;
Matsonia* in 1937. Sold to the Home Lines in 1948
and renamed *Atlantic* in 1949. Engaged in the
Genoa–New York run until reallocated to the
Southampton–Le Havre–Halifax run on February
29, 1952, and to Quebec in place of Halifax on
April 21, 1952. Reverted back to the Mediterran-
ean route in December 1954 when the Home
Lines formed the subsidiary of the National
Hellenic American Line and renamed her *Queen
Frederica*. She entered this service from Piraeus to
Naples, Palermo, Gibraltar, Halifax and New York
on January 29, 1955. Refitted in November
1960–1 at Genoa and her accommodations altered
to 174 first and 1005 tourist class. Sold to the
Chandris Lines in November 1965 and made her
last transatlantic voyage from New York to
Piraeus on September 30, 1967. The *Queen
Frederica* is the oldest liner of her type in service
today and is one of the last remnants of that
wonderful era of luxury liners. Presently in service.

HOMELAND

Builder: Alexander Stephen & Sons Ltd, Glasgow, Scotland.
Completed: April 1905.
Gross tonnage: 10043.
Dimensions: 538ft × 60ft. Depth 41ft.
Engines: Steam turbines, single-reduction geared.
Screws: Triple.
Watertight bulkheads: Seven.
Decks: Four.
Normal speed: 17 knots.
Passenger accommodation: 85 first and 866 tourist class.
Maiden voyage: Genoa–South America on July 27, 1948.

Built for the Allan Line and christened *Virginian.* Sold to the Canadian-Pacific Line in 1916 and retained her original name. Resold to the Swedish-American Line in 1920 and renamed *Drottning-holm.* Resold once again to the Home Lines in April 1948 and renamed *Brasil: Homeland* in June 1951. Engaged in the Genoa–Buenos Aires run, but made five voyages from Naples to New York in the spring of 1950. Reallocated to the Hamburg–Southampton–Cherbourg–Halifax–New York service on June 16, 1951, but reverted back to the Genoa–Naples–New York service in the spring of 1952. Made her last voyage in 1954 and was sold for scrapping at Trieste, Italy, in 1955, but reprieved when she was resold to the South Atlantic Lines the following year and retained until 1962.

Note: She was the first Atlantic liner to be driven by direct-action turbines when constructed as the *Virginian* in 1905, her machinery having been replaced by the presently stated type in 1922 when she was re-engined.

HOMERIC

Builder: Bethlehem Shipbuilding Corp Quincy, Massachusetts, USA.

Completed: December 1931.

Gross tonnage: 18563.

Dimensions: 638ft × 79ft. Depth 45ft.

Engines: Six steam turbines single-reduction geared.

Screws: Twin.

Watertight bulkheads: Eleven.

Decks: Five.

Normal speed: 21 knots. (Attained a speed of 23.50 knots on her trials.)

Passenger accommodation: 147 first and 1096 tourist class.

Maiden voyage: Venice–Mediterranean ports–Halifax–New York on January 24, 1955.

Built for the Matson Lines and christened *Mariposa*. Sold to the Home Lines in November 1953 and renamed *Homeric* in 1954. Engaged in the Naples–New York service until reallocated to the Southampton–Le Havre–Quebec run on May 3, 1955, and since August 12, 1957, from Le Havre to Southampton, Quebec and Montreal. The *Homeric* has made some voyages in conjunction with the *Queen Frederica*. She was refitted at the time of her purchase at Trieste, Italy, at a cost well over $3 million and completed in the course of a twelve-month period. Since October 1963 the *Homeric* has been in a service from New York to the West Indies and Nassau. Presently in service.

ITALIA

Builder: Blohm & Voss, Hamburg, Germany.
Completed: November 1928.
Gross tonnage: 21532.
Dimensions: 609ft × 78ft. Depth 43ft.
Engines: Two eight-cylinder, four-stroke,
   double-acting B & W diesel.
Screws: Twin.
Watertight bulkheads: Ten.
Decks: Five.
Normal speed: 17 knots.
Passenger accommodation: 120 first and
   1320 tourist class.
Maiden voyage: Genoa–South America on
   July 27, 1948.

Built for the Swedish-American Line and christ-ened *Kungsholm*. Sold to the Home Lines in 1947 and renamed *Italia*. Engaged in the Genoa–South American service until June 12, 1949, when she was reverted to the Genoa–Mediterranean ports–New York run. In March 1952 she was transferred once again, this time to the Hamburg–Southamp-ton–Le Havre–Halifax–New York service. Placed in the Cuxhaven – Le Havre – Southampton – Quebec–Montreal run on May 23, 1959. Sold to an American firm in 1964 for conversion to a 500-room hotel at Freeport, Bahamas, and renamed the 'Imperial Bahama Hotel'. Offered up for sale in June 1965 and as no buyers turned up was sold to Spanish shipbreakers in December 1965.

OCEANIC

Builder: Cantieri Riuniti dell' Adriatico,
   Monfalcone, Italy.
Completed: March 1965.
Gross tonnage: 27644.
Dimensions: 782ft × 97ft. Depth 48ft.
Engines: Four steam turbines double-reduction
   geared.
Screws: Twin.
Watertight bulkheads: Thirteen.
Decks: Six.
Normal speed: 26.50 knots.
Officers and crew: 560.
Passenger accommodation: 230 first and
   1370 tourist class. (Accommodations are reduced
   to 1200 when pleasure-cruising.)
Maiden voyage: New York–Bahamas on
   April 24, 1965.

The *Oceanic* was built at a cost of $35 million and is the largest ship ever built especially for cruising. Fully air-conditioned and equipped with Denny-Brown motion stabilisers. She has a fuel capacity of 5400 metric tons and is the Home Line's flagship. Engaged in the New York–Nassau–Bermuda and Bahamas services. Presently in service.

ITALIAN LINE

ANDREA DORIA

Builder: Societa Anonima Ansaldo, Sestri
  Ponente, Genoa, Italy.
Completed: January 1953.
Gross tonnage: 29083.
Dimensions: 700ft × 90ft. Depth 50ft.
Engines: Six steam turbines; high-pressure,
  double-reduction geared; intermediate-
  pressure and low-pressure, single-reduction
  geared.
Screws: Twin.
Watertight bulkheads: Ten.
Decks: Five.
Normal speed: 23 knots.
Passenger accommodation: 218 first, 320
  cabin and 703 tourist class.
Maiden voyage: Genoa—Mediterranean ports—
  New York on January 14, 1953.

Employed in the Genoa—Cannes—Naples—Gibraltar
—New York run. The *Andrea Doria* was rammed
and sunk by the Swedish-American liner
Stockholm in a calm fog at 11.22pm on the
night of July 25, 1956. The *Stockholm* rammed
into the *Doria*'s starboard side where an enor-
mous hole was opened to the sea. She soon gave a
heavy list to port making it almost impossible to
launch the starboard lifeboats and gave way to the
sea, foundering within an hour's time. This
tragedy occurred off the apprehensive Nantucket Shoals where many a ship has been lost
prior to the incident between the *Stockholm* and
the *Andrea Doria* which cost the lives of 52
persons from the Italian liner and five others from
the *Stockholm*. Amongst the first ships to arrive at

the scene was the United Fruit liner *Cape Ann* who
was shortly accompanied by the United States
Army transport *William H. Thomas* and the
French Line's *Ile de France*, the latter which
rescued a considerable complement of her passengers and crew. These three vessels along with
the *Stockholm* with her bow crushed embarked
1565 persons from the sinking liner of only three
years old. Many attempts have been contemplated to raise the *Andrea Doria* which lies in a
depth of 39 fathoms, but none have yet material-
ised to this effect. It has also been mentioned that
in the location where she sank there was great
underwater activity which has probably buried
most of the ship by now.
Sister ship: *Cristoforo Colombo.*

I AUGUSTUS

Builder: Societa Anonima Ansaldo, Cantiere
Navale, Sestri Ponente, Genoa, Italy.
Completed: November 1927.
Gross tonnage: 30418.
Dimensions: 711ft × 83ft. Depth 52ft.
Engines: Four M.A.N. six-cylinder, two-stroke,
double-acting diesel.
Screws: Quadruple.
Watertight bulkheads: Eleven.
Decks: Six.
Normal speed: 19.50 knots.
Passengers and crew: 2700 (approx).

Built for the Navigazione Generale Italiana.
Transferred to the Italian Line on January 2, 1932
upon amalgamation of the NGI and the Lloyd
Sabaudo to form the Italian Line. She was the
largest motor vessel with quadruple screws at the
time of her construction. Employed in the Genoa–
New York service. She was laid up in 1939 and
converted to an aircraft carrier by the Italian Navy
in March 1943 and renamed *Sparviero*. Damaged
by bombing at Genoa on June 26, 1944. She had
been partly dismantled by the Germans when she
was sunk on September 25, 1945. Refloated in
1946 and sold for scrap on July 7, 1947, with
work commencing on August 12, 1947.
Sister ship: *Roma.*

II AUGUSTUS

Builder: Cantieri Riuniti dell' Adriatico, Trieste,
  Italy.
Completed: February 1952.
Gross tonnage: 27090.
Dimensions: 680ft × 49ft. Depth 49ft.
Engines: Two Fiat, twelve-cylinder, two-stroke,
  double-acting diesel.
Screws: Twin.
Watertight bulkheads: Eleven.
Decks: Five.
Normal speed: 21 knots.
Passenger accommodation: 178 first, 288
  cabin and 714 tourist class.
Maiden voyage: Genoa–Mediterranean ports–
  South American ports–Buenos Aires in March
  1952.

Placed in the Genoa–Cannes–Naples–Gibraltar
Halifax–New York run on February 7, 1957.
Reverted to her original service of Genoa–Naples–
Cannes – Barcelona – Lisbon – Funchal – Rio de
Janeiro–Santos–Montevideo–Buenos Aires in

the autumn of 1960. She is equipped with motion
stabilisers and is fully air-conditioned. Presently
in service.
Sister ship: *Il Giulio Cesare.*

COLOMBO

Builder: Palmers Shipbuilding & Iron Co Ltd, Jarrow, England.
Completed: July 1917.
Gross tonnage: 12037.
Dimensions: 536ft × 64ft. Depth 35 ft.
Engines: Two four-cylinder, quadruple expansion.
Screws: Twin.
Watertight bulkheads: Eight.
Decks: Four.
Normal speed: 17 knots.

Built for the Sicula-American Line and christened *San Gennaro*. Sold to the Navigazione Generale Italiana in 1921 and renamed *Colombo*. Passed on to the Italian Line on January 2, 1932, when the NGI and the Lloyd Sabaudo merged to form the Italian Line. Engaged in the Genoa–South American trade. Sold to the Lloyd Triestino in 1937 and sunk off Massawa, Ethiopia on April 4, 1941. She was later raised and scrapped.

CONTE BIANCAMANO

Builder: William Beardmore & Co Ltd, Glasgow,
  Scotland.
Completed: November 1925.
Gross tonnage: 23562.
Dimensions: 665ft × 76ft. Depth 48ft.
Engines: Four steam turbines double-reduction
  geared.
Screws: Twin.
Collision bulkhead: One
Watertight bulkheads: Nine.
Decks: Five.
Normal speed: 20 knots.
Passenger accommodation: 215 first, 333
  cabin and 1030 tourist class.

Employed in the Genoa—Mediterranean ports—
South American trade. In 1935 she did some troop
work to Ethiopia during the Italian invasion of
East Africa. In 1937 she was sold to the Lloyd
Triestino. Seized by the United States at Colon,
Panama in March 1941 and renamed *Hermitage*
for use as a transport. Returned to Italy in 1947
and reconditioned with two new funnels to replace the old ring-topped type and her raked stem

curved. She was now under the ownership of the
Societa Marittima Nazionale. Chartered by the
Italian Line and resumed services on November 10,
1949 from Genoa to Buenos Aires. The *Conte
Biancamano* was now in the intermediate North
and South American trades and worked the
Genoa—Naples—Barcelona—Lisbon—Halifax—New
York run. Sold for scrap in Italy in October 1960.
Sister ship: *Conte Grande*.

CONTE DI SAVOIA

Builder: Cantieri Ruiniti dell' Adriatico, Trieste, Italy.
Completed: November 1932.
Gross tonnage: 48502.
Dimensions: 860ft × 96ft. Depth 53ft.
Engines: Twelve steam turbines, single-reduction geared.
Screws: Quadruple.
Watertight bulkheads: Twelve.
Decks: Six.
Normal speed: 27.50 knots. (Attained a speed of 30 knots on her trials.)
Passenger accommodation: 360 first, 778 tourist and 922 third class.
Maiden voyage: Genoa–New York on November 30, 1932.

The keel was laid down for the Lloyd Sabaudo and was to be named *Conte Azzuro*. Passed on to Italian Line ownership when the Lloyd Sabaudo and the Navigazione Generale Italiana consolidated to form the Italian Line on January 2, 1932. Employed in the Genoa–New York run year-round. *Conti di Savoia* was one of the first liners to be equipped with Sperry gyro stabilisers which reduced the roll to less than two and a half degrees in the worst weather. On her maiden voyage she was held up 800 miles outside of New York by a broken exhaust valve which blew a hole in her hull plating. The damage was repaired and she lost only a day's time. The *Conte di Savoia*'s upper deck was 460 ft long. Withdrawn from service in 1939 and laid up until 1943 when she did some troop work. Laid up again at Malamocco, Venice, where she was disguised as an island. Attacked by US fighter bombers who scored six hits on September 11, 1943. Refloated on October 16, 1945, with the intention of reconstructing her, but speculating as too costly to repair was sold for scrap at Monfalcone, Italy, in 1950.

CONTE GRANDE

Builder: Stabilimento Tecnico, Trieste, Italy.
Completed: February 1928.
Gross tonnage: 23842.
Dimensions: 667ft × 78ft. Depth 48ft.
Engines: Four steam turbines, double-reduction geared.
Screws: Twin.
Collision bulkhead: One.
Watertight bulkheads: Nine.
Decks: Five.
Normal speed: 20 knots.
Officers and crew: 532.
Passenger accommodation: 215 first, 333 cabin and 950 tourist class.
Maiden voyage for Lloyd Sabaudo: Genoa —Naples—New York, arriving on April 14, 1928.

Built for the Lloyd Sabaudo, Transferred to the Italian Line on January 2, 1932 upon amalgamation of the Lloyd Sabaudo and the Navigazione Generale Italiana. Engaged in the Genoa–South American trade. Requisitioned for troop work to East Africa in October 1935 and later resumed regular sailings. Seized by Brazil on August 22, 1941, and sold to the United States who converted her into a troopship under the name of *Monticello* in 1942. Returned to the Italian Government on July 23, 1947, and reconditioned. Her two funnels were replaced by a modern pair and was placed under the ownership of the Societa Marittima Nazionale.

Chartered to the Italian Line and resumed sailings on July 14, 1949, from Genoa to Buenos Aires. The *Conte Grande* was now interchangeable in the North and South American trades and worked the Naples–Genoa–Cannes–Rio de Janeiro–River Plate service after her last voyage to New York from Genoa via Cannes and Naples on September 25, 1956. Withdrawn from service in late 1960 and made one voyage to Australia for the Lloyd Triestino in December 1960. Sold for scrap at Spezia, Italy, in September 1961 and broken up by June 1962.
Sister ship: *Conte Biancamano.*

CRISTOFORO COLOMBO

Builder: Societa Anonima Ansaldo, Sestri Ponente, Genoa, Italy.
Completed: July 1954.
Gross tonnage: 29429.
Dimensions: 701ft × 90ft. Depth 50ft.
Engines: Six steam turbines; high-pressure, double-reduction geared; intermediate-pressure and low-pressure, single-reduction geared.
Screws: Twin.
Watertight bulkheads: Ten.
Decks: Five.
Normal speed: 23 knots. (Attained a speed of 26.50 knots on her trial runs.)
Passenger accommodation: 229 first, 222 cabin and 604 tourist class.
Maiden voyage: Genoa—Mediterranean ports—New York on July 15, 1954.
Last voyage: Lisbon—Malaga—Cannes—Genoa—Naples—Palermo—Messina—Piraeus—Venice—Trieste on January 20, 1973.

Employed in the Genoa—Cannes—Naples—Gibraltar—Halifax—New York run until June 1960 when she was diverted to the Trieste—Venice—Piraeus—Messina — Palermo — Naples — Malaga — Lisbon — Halifax—New York run with calls at Boston and Ponta Delgada, Azores, on occasion eastbound and Halifax westbound only. Equipped with motion stabilisers and fully air-conditioned. The *Colombo* has three swimming pools and three separate dining rooms for her three classes. One of the few liners with a truly extensive and interesting itinerary. *(See Notes on p. 223.)*
Sister ship: *Andrea Doria*.

DONIZETTI

Builder: Cantieri Riuniti dell' Adriatico,
Trieste, Italy.
Completed: April 1951.
Gross tonnage: 13226.
Dimensions: 528ft × 69ft. Depth 42ft.
Engines: Two ten-cylinder, two-stroke, single-
acting Sulzer diesel.
Screws: Twin.
Watertight bulkheads: Nine.
Decks: Four.
Normal speed: 18 knots.
Passenger accommodation: 160 first and 440
tourist class.

Built for the Lloyd Triestino and christened
Australia. Bartered to the Italian Line for another
ship in the spring of 1963 and renamed *Donizetti*.
Employed in the Genoa–Naples–Cannes–Bar-
celona–Tenerife–La Guaira–Curaçao–Cartagena–
Cristobal–Buena Ventura–Guayaquil–Callo–Arica
–Antofagasta–Valparaiso service. Equipped with
motion stabilisers and fully air-conditioned.
(See Notes on p. 223.)
Sister ships: *Rossini* and *Verdi*.

DUILIO

Builder: Societa Anonima Ansaldo, Sestri Ponente, Genoa, Italy.
Completed: October 1923.
Gross tonnage: 23635.
Dimensions: 636ft × 76ft. Depth 50ft.
Engines: Four direct-action steam turbines.
Screws: Quadruple.
Watertight bulkheads: Fifteen.
Decks: Five.
Normal speed: 21 knots.
Passenger accommodation: 280 first, 670 second and 600 third class.
Maiden voyage for the NGI: Genoa—New York, arriving on November 9, 1923.

Built for the Navigazione Generale Italiana. Transferred to the Italian Line on January 2, 1932, upon amalgamation of the NGI and the Lloyd Sabaudo to form the Italian Line. Employed in the Genoa–South American trade until she was diverted to the Genoa–Capetown service after being over-hauled in September 1933. Sold to the Lloyd Triestino in 1937. She was utilised by the Italians as a hospital ship during World War II and her cabin fittings were partly removed by the Germans in June 1944. Sunk by allied aircraft at Trieste on July 10, 1944. Found capsized by the allies in May 1945 and sold for scrap in 1948 with work commencing on February 11.
Sister ship: *Giulio Cesare*.

I GIULIO CESARE

Builder: Swan, Hunter & Wigham Richardson
Ltd, Wallsend-on-Tyne, England.
Completed: November 1921.
Gross tonnage: 21900.
Dimensions: 636ft × 76ft. Depth 50ft.
Engines: Four steam turbines, single-reduction
geared.
Screws: Quadruple.
Watertight bulkheads: Fifteen
Decks: Five.
Normal speed: 19 knots.
Passenger accommodation: 259 first, 328 sec-
ond, and 1706 third class.
Maiden voyage for the NGI: Genoa—New York, ar-
riving on August 22, 1922.

Built for the Navigazione Generale Italiana. Transferred to the Italian Line on January 2, 1932, when
the NGI and the Lloyd Sabaudo amalgamated to
form the Italian Line. Engaged in the Genoa—
South American trade until reconditioned in
November 1933 and placed in the Genoa—
Capetown service. Sold to the Lloyd Triestino in
1937. Her cabin fittings were partly removed by
the Germans in June 1944 and she was sunk by
allied aircraft at Trieste on September 11, 1944.
Found capsized by the allies in May 1945 and sold
for scrap in 1948 with work commencing on
February 11. She was scrapped under the name of
Achille Lauro, though no evidence is available as
to when she was renamed.
Sister ship: *Duilio.*

II GIULIO CESARE

Builder: Cantieri dell' Adriatico, Monfalcone, Italy.
Completed: September 1951.
Gross tonnage: 27078.
Dimensions: 681ft × 88ft. Depth 49ft.
Engines: Two Fiat twelve-cylinder, two-stroke double-acting diesel.
Screws: Twin.
Watertight bulkheads: Eleven.
Decks: Five.
Normal speed: 21 knots.
Passenger accommodation: 178 first, 288 cabin and 714 tourist class.
Maiden voyage: Venice–Mediterranean ports–South American ports–Buenos Aires on October 27, 1951.

Transferred to the Genoa–Cannes–Naples–Gibraltar–Halifax–New York service on June 29, 1956. Diverted to her original service of Genoa–Naples–Cannes–Barcelona–Lisbon–Funchal–Rio de Janeiro–Santos–Montevideo–Buenos Aires. Equipped with motion stabilisers and fully air-conditioned. Currently in service.
Sister ship: *Augustus*.

LEONARDO DA VINCI

Builder: Ansaldo SpA. Cantiere Navale, Sestri, Genoa, Italy.
Completed: June 1960.
Gross tonnage: 33340.
Dimensions: 767ft × 92ft. Depth 51ft.
Engines: Four steam turbines, double-reduction geared.
Screws: Twin.
Watertight bulkheads: Fourteen.
Decks: Five.
Normal speed: 25.50 knots.
Passenger accommodation: 413 first, 342 cabin and 571 tourist class.
Maiden voyage: Genoa–Cannes–Naples–New York on June 30, 1960.
Last voyage for Italian Line: Genoa–Naples –Rhodes–Beirut–Alexandria (a cruise) on September 19, 1976.

Employed in the Naples–Palermo–Genoa–Barcelona–Algeciras–Lisbon–Halifax–New York service with a call at Palma in place of Barcelona eastbound and Halifax only westbound. The *Leonardo da Vinci* also cruises to the West Indies during the off-seasonal months and makes special long cruises. She was built to replace the loss of the *Andrea Doria* and was designed so as to be converted to nuclear propulsion at a later date. Equipped with motion stabilisers and fully air-conditioned. *(See Notes on p. 223.)*

MICHELANGELO

Builder: Cantieri Riuniti dell' Adriatico,
Trieste, Italy.
Completed: April 1965.
Gross tonnage: 45911.
Dimensions: 905ft × 102ft. Depth 52ft.
Engines: Four steam turbines double-reduction
geared.
Screws: Twin.
Watertight bulkheads: Sixteen.
Decks: Six.
Normal speed: 25.50 knots. (Attained a speed
of 29.15 knots during her trials.)
Passenger accommodation: 535 first, 550
cabin and 690 tourist class.
Maiden voyage: Genoa—Cannes—Naples—New
York on May 12, 1965.
Officers and crew: 720.
Last voyage for Italian Line: New York—Algeciras
—Naples—Cannes—Genoa on June 26, 1975.

Employed in the Genoa—Cannes—Naples—Algeciras—New York run with cruises to the West Indies during the off season. On April 12, 1966, the *Michelangelo* encountered 35ft waves while *en route* from Genoa to New York. The ship hove to for hours with her engines shut down and sustained heavy damages when her bow was nearly crumpled by a 50ft wave. Much damage was also done by the waves which smashed 40ft of bulwark and railing from her bridge, sweeping overboard three persons of the 775 on board. Her funnels are constructed of fibre glass and she has a bulbous bow to increase her speed. In 1966 new propellers were fitted and she attained a new speed of 31.59 knots on trials. Fully air-conditioned and equipped with motion stabilisers she is the Italian Line's flagship. *(See Notes on p. 223.)*
Sister ship: *Raffaello.*

NEPTUNIA

Builder: Cantieri Riuniti dell' Adriatico,
   Monfalcone, Italy.
Completed: September 1932.
Gross tonnage: 19475.
Dimensions: 590ft × 76ft. Depth 46ft.
Engines: Two eight-cylinder and two nine-
   cylinder, two-stroke, single acting Sulzer diesel.
Screws: Quadruple.
Watertight bulkheads: Ten.
Decks: Four.
Normal speed: 19 knots. (Attained a speed of
   21.08 knots on her trial runs.)
Passenger accommodation: 175 cabin and
   709 third class.
Maiden voyage: Naples—Buenos Aires on October
   7, 1932.

Built for the Cosulich Line. Transferred to the Italian Line in January 1935 upon absorption of the Cosulich Line. Engaged in the Genoa—via Suez Canal—Bombay—Shanghai service from February 1935 onwards. Sunk by a British submarine in the Mediterranean while *en route* from Taranto, Italy, to Tripoli, Lybia, with troops on September 18, 1941.
Sister ship: *Oceania*.

OCEANIA

Builder: Cantieri Riuniti dell' Adriatico, Monfalcone, Italy.
Completed: July 1933.
Gross tonnage: 19507.
Dimensions: 590ft × 77ft. Depth 46ft.
Engines: Four Fiat eight-cylinder, two-stroke, single-acting diesel.
Screws: Quadruple.
Watertight bulkheads: Ten.
Decks: Four.
Normal speed: 19 knots. (Attained a speed of 22.12 knots during her trials.)
Officers and crew: 250.
Passenger accommodation: 200 cabin, 400 third and 650 steerage.
Maiden voyage: Trieste–Buenos Aires on April 6, 1933.

Built for the Cosulich Line. Transferred to the Italian Line in January 1935 upon absorption of the Cosulich Line. Employed in the Genoa–via Suez Canal–Bombay–Shanghai service from February 1935 onwards. Sunk by a British submarine in the Mediterranean on April 9, 1941, while transporting troops.
Sister ship: *Neptunia*.

ORAZIO

Builder: Cantieri ed Officine, Meridionale, Baia, Italy.
Gross tonnage: 11669
Dimensions: 506ft × 62ft. Depth 36ft.
Engines: Two eight-cylinder, four-stroke, single-acting diesel.
Screws: Twin.
Watertight bulkheads: Nine.
Decks: Four.
Normal speed: 14 knots.
Passenger accommodation: 110 first, 190 second and 340 third class.
Completed: October 1927.

Built for the Navigazione Generale Italiana. Transferred to the Italian Line on January 2, 1932, upon amalgamation of the NGI and the Lloyd Sabaudo. Engaged in the Genoa–Mediterranean ports–Central & South American–Valparaiso service. Burned outside of Marseilles, France while *en route* from Genoa to Valparaiso after an explosion and was abandoned on January 21, 1940. *(See Notes on p. 223.)*
Sister ship: *Virgilio.*

RAFFAELLO

Builder: Cantieri Riuniti dell' Adriatico, Monfalcone, Italy.

Completed: July 1965.

Gross tonnage: 45933.

Dimensions: 905ft × 102ft. Depth 52ft.

Engines: Four steam turbines, double-reduction geared.

Screws: Twin.

Watertight bulkheads: Sixteen.

Decks: Six.

Normal speed: 26.50 knots. (Attained a speed of 30.15 knots on her trials.)

Passenger accommodation: 535 first, 550 cabin and 690 tourist class.

Maiden voyage: Genoa–Cannes–Naples–New York on July 18, 1965.

Last voyage: New York–Algeciras–Naples–Cannes–Genoa on April 21, 1975.

Employed in the Genoa–Cannes–Naples–Algeciras–New York service with cruises to the West Indies during the off season. Her funnels are constructed of fibre glass and she has a bulbous bow to increase her speed. *(See Notes on p. 223.)*

Sister ship: *Michelangelo.*

REX

Builder: Societa Anonima Ansaldo, Sestri Ponente, Genoa, Italy.
Completed: September 1932.
Gross tonnage: 51062.
Dimensions: 880ft × 97ft. Depth 61ft.
Engines: Twelve steam turbines, single-reduction geared.
Screws: Quadruple.
Watertight bulkheads: Fourteen.
Decks: Six.
Normal speed: 28 knots. (Attained a speed of 28.90 knots on her trials.)
Officers and crew: 810.
Passenger accommodation: 378 first, 378 second, 410 tourist and 866 third class.
Maiden voyage: Genoa–New York on September 27, 1932.

The keel was laid down for the Navigazione Generale Italiana and was to be named *Guglielmo Marconi*. Passed on to Italian Line ownership when the NGI and the Lloyd Sabaudo merged on January 2, 1932, to form the Italian Line. Employed in the Genoa–New York run year-round. The *Rex*'s maiden voyage was marred by trouble with her turbo dynamos which caused her to put in at Gibraltar for repairs that lasted three days. Many of her passengers left for other means of transportation during the incident and the *Rex* steamed into New York harbour an embarrassed ship. In August 1933 she more than made up for the mishap on her maiden voyage by making the run from Tarifa Point to Ambrose Lighthouse in 4 days, 13 hours and 58 minutes at a speed of 28.92 knots and won the Blue Riband from the North German Lloyd's *Bremen*. In March 1937 she experienced one of her worst passages when she was

caught in a gale between the Azores and Cape Vincent. One crew member was killed when an immense wave struck causing the ship to list 20 degrees and injuring several passengers. The *Rex* had an upper deck 619ft long. Laid up at Bari, Italy. in October 1939. On September 8, 1944, she was attacked by British Beaufighters who scored 123 hits on the *Rex* and sank her in low water where she lay on her port side just outside of Capo d'Istria, Trieste, Italy. Refloated in 1947 with the hope of salvaging the remaining hulk, the *Rex* lay in a part of the harbour now belonging to Yugoslavia and to the discretion of the Slavs it was decided to sell her for scrap. Broken up at Trieste in July 1947 whereby work commenced on July 30. The *Rex* was the only Italian liner ever to win the Blue Riband and was along with her running mate the *Conte de Savoia* one of the best looking ships ever to wear the colours of the Italian Line.

ROMA

Builder: Societa Anonima Ansaldo, Sestri
Ponente, Genoa, Italy.
Completed: September 1926.
Gross tonnage: 30816.
Dimensions: 710ft × 83ft. Depth 52ft.
Engines: Eight steam turbines, single-
reduction geared.
Screws: Quadruple.
Watertight bulkheads: Twelve.
Decks: Six.
Normal speed: 19 knots.
Maiden voyage for the NGI: Genoa—New York, ar-
riving on October 1, 1926.
Passenger accommodation: 281 first, 672 second,
and 737 third class.

Built for the Navigazione Generale Italiana. Transferred to the Italian Line on January 2, 1932, when
the NGI and the Lloyd Sabaudo consolidated to
form the Italian Line. Engaged in the Genoa—New
York service and in 1933 was reallocated to the
Genoa—Capetown route. Acquired by the Italian
Navy in October 1940 and renamed *Aquila* in
1943. Her cabin fittings were being removed by
the Germans when she was damaged by five
direct hits by allied aircraft at Genoa on June 20,
1944, when nearly completed as an aircraft
carrier. Bombed and sunk at Genoa on July 14,
1945. She was refloated and scrapped at Spezia.
Italy, in 1950.
Sister ship: *Augustus.*

ROSSINI

Builder: Cantieri Riuniti dell' Adriatico, Trieste, Italy.
Completed: September 1951.
Gross tonnage: 13225.
Dimensions: 528ft × 69ft. Depth 42ft.
Engines: Two ten-cylinder, two-stroke, single-acting Sulzer diesel.
Screws: Twin:
Watertight bulkheads: Nine.
Decks: Four.
Normal speed: 17.50 knots.
Passenger accommodation: 103 first and 446 tourist class.
Officers and crew: 236.

Built for the Lloyd Triestino and christened *Neptunia*. Bartered to the Italian Line in the spring of 1963 and renamed *Rossini*. Engaged in the Genoa – Naples – Cannes – Barcelona – Tenerife – La Guaira – Curaçao – Cartagena – Cristobal – Buena Ventura – Guayaquil – Callo – Arica – Antofagasta – Valparaiso service. Equipped with motion stabilisers and fully air-conditioned. Presently in service.
Sister ships: *Donizetti* and *Verdi*.

SARDEGNA

Builder: Bremer Vulkan, Vegesack, Germany.
Completed: May 1923.
Gross tonnage: 11452.
Dimensions: 512ft × 66ft. Depth 34ft.
Engines: Two three-cylinder, triple expansion.
Screws: Twin.
Watertight bulkheads: Nine.
Decks: Four.
Normal speed: 14 knots.

Built for the North German Lloyd and christened *Sierra Ventana*. Sold to the Italian Line in 1935 and renamed *Sardegna*. Engaged in the Genoa– South American trade until sold to the Lloyd Triestino in 1937. Sunk by an allied submarine in December 1940.

SATURNIA

Builder: Cantiere Navale Triestino, Monfalcone, Italy.
Completed: September 1927.
Gross tonnage: 24346
Dimensions: 651ft × 80ft. Depth 47ft.
Engines: Two ten-cylinder, two-stroke, double-acting Sulzer diesel.
Screws: Twin.
Collision bulkhead: One.
Watertight bulkheads: Nine.
Decks: Five.
Normal speed: 21 knots.
Passenger accommodation: 240 first, 270 cabin and 860 tourist class.

Built for the Cosulich Line. Transferred to the Italian Line in January 1935 upon absorption of the Cosulich Line. Employed in the Trieste–Mediterranean ports–New York run. In 1935 her former B & W eight-cylinder, four-stroke diesel engines were replaced by the presently stated type of propulsion. Requisitioned for troop service to East Africa on August 24, 1935, and later by the United States in 1943 after Italy's surrender to the allies and was used as a hospital ship under the name of *Francis Y. Slanger*. Returned to the Italian Line in December 1946 and recovered her original name. Resumed transatlantic sailings on August 29, 1947, after some alterations and worked out of Naples for a time until she was later based at her home port of Trieste and worked to Venice–Patras–Naples–Palermo–Gibraltar–Lisbon –Halifax–New York on November 8, 1955. Withdrawn from service in April 1965 and laid up at Trieste pending her disposal which came about in October when she was sold to shipbreakers in Italy.
Sister ship: *Vulcania.*

VERDI

Builder: Cantieri Riuniti dell' Adriatico, Trieste, Italy.

Completed: August 1951.

Gross tonnage: 13226.

Dimensions: 529ft × 69ft. Depth 42ft.

Engines: Two ten-cylinder, two-stroke, single-acting Sulzer diesel.

Screws: Twin.

Watertight bulkheads: Nine.

Decks: Four.

Normal speed: 17.50 knots.

Passenger accommodation: 103 first and 446 tourist class.

Officers and crew: 236.

Built for the Lloyd Triestino and christened *Oceania*. Bartered to the Italian Line in the spring of 1963 for another vessel and renamed *Verdi*. Employed in the Genoa–Naples–Cannes–Barcelona–Tenerife–La Guaira–Curaçao–Cartagena –Cristobal–Buena Ventura–Guayaquil–Callo–Arica –Antofagasta–Valparaiso service. Equipped with motion stabilisers and fully air-conditioned. Presently in service.

Sister ships: *Donizetti* and *Rossini*.

VIRGILIO

Builder: Cantieri ed Officine, Meridionali, Baia, Italy.
Completed: April 1928.
Gross tonnage: 11718.
Dimensions: 506ft × 62ft. Depth 36ft.
Engines: Two eight-cylinder, four-stroke, single-acting diesel.
Screws: Twin.
Normal speed: 14 knots.
Passenger accommodation: 110 first, 190 second and 340 third class.

Built for the Navigazione Generale Italiana. Transferred to the Italian Line on January 2, 1932, upon amalgamation of the NGI and the Lloyd Sabaudo. Employed in the Genoa—Mediterranean ports—Central & South American ports—Valparaiso service. Seized by the Germans at Toulon, France, after Italy's surrender in September 1943. She was damaged by a torpedo attack in December 1943 and obstructing the entrance into Toulon harbour was scuttled by the Germans in June 1944.
Sister ship: *Orazio.*

VULCANIA

Builder: Cantiere Navale Triestino, Monfalcone, Italy.
Completed: December 1928.
Gross tonnage: 24496.
Dimensions: 652ft × 80ft. Depth 47ft.
Engines: Two Fiat ten-cylinder, two-stroke, double-acting diesel.
Screws: Twin.
Collision bulkhead: One.
Watertight bulkheads: Nine.
Decks: Five.
Normal speed: 21 knots. (Attained a speed of 23.33 knots on her trials.)
Passenger accommodation: 240 first, 270 cabin and 860 tourist class.
Maiden voyage for Cosulich Line: Trieste—Patras—Palermo—Naples—New York, arriving on December 31, 1928.
Last voyage for Italian Line: New York—Lisbon — Gibraltar — Palermo — Naples — Patras—Venice—Trieste on April 21, 1965.

Built for the Cosulich Line. Transferred to the Italian Line in January 1935 after absorption of the Cosulich Line. Employed in the Trieste–Mediterranean ports–New York service. In 1935 her former B & W eight-cylinder, four-stroke diesel engines were replaced by the presently stated type of propulsion. Commandeered by the United States in 1943 for troop work and was returned back to the Italian Line after having been decommissioned on December 14, 1946. She resumed scheduled sailings from Genoa to Naples and New York after reconditioning on January 20, 1947. Reverted back to her home port at Trieste on October 28, 1955, and worked to Venice–Patras–Naples–Palermo–Gibraltar–Lisbon Halifax–New York. Withdrawn from service in May 1965 and laid up at Trieste until sold to the Sicula Oceanica in late 1965 and renamed *Caribia. (See Notes on p. 223.)*
Sister ship: *Saturnia.*

NORTH GERMAN LLOYD

BARBAROSA

Builder: Blohm & Voss, Hamburg, Germany.
Completed: 1896.
Gross tonnage: 10984.
Dimensions: 526ft × 60ft. Depth 35ft.
Engines: Two four-cylinder, quadruple expansion.
Screws: Twin.
Decks: Four.
Normal speed: 13.50 knots.
Passenger accommodation: 114 first, 175 second, 252 third and 1832 steerage.

Employed in the Bremen–Southampton–New York run during the summer season and from Bremen to Southampton, Suez Canal, Adelaide, Melbourne and Sydney in the winter months. Commenced her last voyage to Australia from Bremen to Southampton, Suez Canal, Adelaide, Melbourne and Sydney on December 25, 1910. Interned at the port of New York at the outbreak of World War I and seized by the United States Government upon America's entry into the war in April 1917. She was converted to a transport and renamed *Mercury*. Witheld by the United States after the war and laid up until sold for scrap in 1924.
Sister ship: *Bremen*.

II BERLIN

Builder: A.G. Weser, Bremen, Germany.
Completed: 1908.
Gross tonnage: 17324.
Dimensions: 613ft × 70ft. Depth 39ft.
Engines: Two four-cylinder quadruple expansion.
Screws: Twin.
Watertight bulkheads: Ten.
Decks: Four.
Normal speed: 17 knots.
Passenger accommodation: 266 first, 246 second and 2700 steerage.

Employed in the Genoa–New York service and ran from Bremen to New York from June until September of each year. Converted to a minelayer in August 1914. The *Berlin* is alleged to have planted the mine that sunk the British battleship *Audacious* off the Ulster coast of Ireland on October 26, 1914. She was interned at Trondheim, Norway, on November 17, 1914. Allocated to Britain in 1919 and managed by the P & O Line until sold by the British Shipping Controller to the White Star Line in November 1920 and renamed *Arabic*. In 1926 she ran for the closely affiliated Red Star Line. Reverted back to the White Star Line in 1930 and was sold for scrap at Genoa, Italy, in December 1931.
Sister ship: *Prinz Friedrich Wilhelm*.

III BERLIN

Builder: Bremer Vulkan, Vegesack, Germany.
Completed: March 1925.
Gross tonnage: 15286.
Dimensions: 572ft × 69ft. Depth 39ft.
Engines: Two four-cylinder, triple expansion.
Screws: Twin.
Decks: Four.
Normal speed: 16.50 knots.
Passenger accommodation: 257 cabin, 261 tourist and 361 third class.
Maiden voyage: Bremen—Southampton—New York on September 26, 1925.

Employed in the Bremen—Southampton—Cherbourg—New York run. On November 12, 1928, the *Berlin* rescued a number of people from the sinking Lamport & Holt liner *Vestris*, the latter *en route* from New York to Barbados. Chartered by the Nazis in 1939 as a worker's cruising ship and was later used as a hospital ship during the war. At one time she was used to repatriate Germans from European ports to the fatherland. Sunk by a mine off Swinemünde Bay, Poland, on February 1, 1945. Refloated and salved by the Russians in 1949 and renamed *Admiral Nakhimov*. She re-entered in their services in 1957 and is presently in operation for the Baltic Steamship Company.

IV BERLIN

Builder: W. G. Armstrong, Whitworth & Co Ltd, Newcastle-on-Tyne, England.
Completed: November 1925.
Gross tonnage: 18600.
Dimensions: 590ft × 74ft. Depth 43ft.
Engines: Two six-cylinder, four-stroke, double-acting Burmeister & Wain diesel.
Screws: Twin.
Watertight bulkheads: Ten.
Decks: Five.
Normal speed: 15.50 knots.
Passenger accommodation: 98 first and 878 tourist class.
Maiden voyage: Bremerhaven–New York on January 8, 1955.

Built for the Swedish-American Line and christened *Gripsholm*. Sold to the Bremen-Amerika Line on January 30, 1954 and subsequently passed to the North German Lloyd with the Swedish-American Line still retaining half ownership. North German Lloyd assumed full ownership in January 1955 and renamed her *Berlin*. Engaged in the Bremerhaven–Southampton–Cherbourg–Halifax–New York run and cruising. The *Berlin* was the first transatlantic liner to be driven by diesel engines when constructed as the *Gripsholm* and the first to inaugurate German passenger service to the United States since 1939. The *Berlin* did not call at Southampton until June 1960 and calls at Halifax westbound only. Sold to Italian shipbreakers in October 1966.

Note: She made her first voyage on February 1, 1954, but was not completely owned by the North German Lloyd and sailed under the name of *Gripsholm*.

11 BREMEN

Builder: F. Schichau, Danzig, Germany,
Completed: May 1897.
Gross tonnage: 11540.
Dimensions: 569ft × 60ft. Depth 35ft.
Engines: Two four-cylinder, quadruple
  expansion.
Screws: Twin.
Decks: Four.
Normal speed: 15.50 knots.
Passenger accommodation: 345 first, 314
  second and 1699 steerage.
Officers and crew: 250.
Maiden voyage: Bremen—New York on June 5,
  1897.
Last voyage for North German Lloyd Line: New
  York—Bremen on July 4, 1914.

Engaged in the Bremen—Southampton—via Suez Canal—Adelaide—Melbourne—Sydney trade and made her last such voyage on October 1, 1911 when she was reallocated to the Bremen—New York run permanently. She was present at the great dock fire at Hoboken, New Jersey, on June 30, 1900, and was seriously damaged. Repaired and her length increased from 525ft to 550ft registered length. The *Bremen* had been in an

interchangeable service between New York and the Far East. Allotted to the British in 1919 as a World War I reparation and transferred to the P & O Line for management until sold to the Byron Steamship Co in 1921 and renamed *Constantinople: King Alexander* in 1923. Sold for scrap in Italy in July 1929.
Sister ship: *Barbarosa.*

IV BREMEN

Builder: A.G. Weser, Bremen, Germany.
Completed: 1929.
Gross tonnage: 51731.
Dimensions: 938ft×102ft. Depth 48ft.
Engines: Twelve steam turbines, single-reduction geared.
Screws: Quadruple.
Watertight bulkheads: Fourteen.
Decks: Seven.
Normal speed: 27.50 knots. (She attained a speed of 28.50 knots on her trial runs.)
Officers and crew: 944.
Passenger accommodation: 723 first, 600 tourist and 908 third class.
Maiden voyage: Bremen—Southampton—Cherbourg—New York on July 16, 1929.

The *Bremen* won the Blue Riband from the Cunard Line's *Mauretania* on her maiden voyage by making the run from Cherbourg to Ambrose Lighthouse in 4 days, 17 hours and 42 minutes at a speed of 27.83 knots. She was the first ship to be built with a bulbous bow created by her German designers to increase her speed. Her hull plating was also built in a paradoxical way that was forward to aft overlapping, a method that was to increase speed by half a knot. Engaged in the Bremen—Southampton—Cherbourg—New York run. The *Bremen* consumed 830 tons of oil every 24 hours and she was equipped with anti-rolling tanks. Her funnels were later raised 15ft because of lingering smoke exhausts on the boat deck. In February 1939 the *Bremen* passed through the Panama Canal while on a pleasure cruise around the continent of South America and is the largest ship ever to pass through the canal. Anticipating war between Great Britain and Germany the *Bremen* slipped out of New York on the night of August 30, 1939 without passengers and made for the port of Murmansk, Russia, by way of Scotland and Norway, thus avoiding the English Channel. She arrived at Murmansk on September 6 and proceeded on to Bremen on December 10. During this elusive voyage she had been spotted by the British submarine *Salmon*, but was fortunate to escape from being sunk. On March 18, 1941, the majestic *Bremen* was set afire by one of her crew members and was scuttled. She was later stripped down to the waterline and the remainder of the hulk was broken up by 1953.
Sister ship: *Europa*.

V BREMEN

Builder: Chantiers & Ateliers de Penhoet, St Nazaire, France.

Completed: August 1939.

Gross tonnage: 32360.

Dimensions: 697ft × 90ft. Depth 48ft.

Engines: Four Parson steam turbines, single-reduction geared.

Screws: Quadruple.

Decks: Five.

Normal speed: 23.50 knots.

Officers and crew: 544.

Passenger accommodation: 1034 tourist class.

Maiden voyage: Bremerhaven–Southampton–Cherbourg–New York on July 9, 1959.

Last voyage for North German Lloyd Line: Bremerhaven–Southampton–Funchal–Dakar–Sao Vicente – Las Palmas – Lisbon – Southampton –Bremerhaven (a cruise) on December 27, 1971.

Built for the Compagnie Sud-Atlantique and christened *Pasteur*. Sold to North German Lloyd in September 1957 and renamed *Bremen* in 1959 after almost being completely rebuilt. Employed in the Bremerhaven – Southampton – Cherbourg – New York run with some cruising during the year to the West Indies. The *Bremen* was purchased for £2 million and refitted at a cost of about £6million. She is the North German Lloyd's flagship and is currently in operation. On September 1, 1970, She passed on to a joint ownership between the North German Lloyd and the Hamburg-America Line when the two merged. Each Line holds an equal amount of stock in the new company which is now known as Hapag-Lloyd. It must be noted that the name North German Lloyd is still used in relation to the *Bremen*.

(See Notes on p. 223.)

II COLUMBUS

Builder: F. Schichau, Danzig, Germany.
Completed: November 1923.
Gross tonnage: 32581.
Dimensions: 775ft × 83ft. Depth 49ft.
Engines: Two single-reduction geared turbines.
Screws: Twin.
Decks: Five.
Normal speed: 23 knots.
Passenger accommodation: 478 cabin, 644
   tourist and 602 third class.
Officers and crew: 576.
Maiden voyage: Bremen—New York on April 22,
   1924.
Last voyage for North German Lloyd Line: New
   York—Curacao—San Juan—Havana (a cruise) on
   August 19, 1939.

Laid down as the *Hindenburg* in 1914 it was later
decided to give her the name of the former surrendered vessel *Columbus* before launching in 1918.
Construction was held up during the war and she
was not completed until June 1922. In 1929 her
funnels were replaced by shorter ones of greater
diameter making her appear somewhat like the
Bremen and *Europa*. At the time of this refit she
was converted from coal-firing to oil and her
reciprocating machinery replaced by the presently stated type of propulsion. Re-entered service in May 1930 and made a world cruise that
year. Employed in the Bremen—Southampton—
New York run with a call at Plymouth in place of
Southampton eastbound. When World War II
broke out she was running from New York to the
West Indies. On December 19, 1939, she was inter-
cepted by the British cruiser *Hyperion* when
attempting to sail for the fatherland. She was
scuttled by her crew to avoid capture 300 miles off
the Virginian coast.

II DRESDEN

Builder: Bremer Vulkan, Vegesack, Germany.
Completed: January 1915.
Gross tonnage: 14690.
Dimensions: 550ft × 67ft. Depth 39ft.
Engines: Two four-cylinder, quadruple
  expansion.
Screws: Twin.
Watertight bulkheads: Thirteen.
Decks: Four.
Normal speed: 15 knots.
Passenger accommodation: 319 first, 156 second,
  342 third, and 1348 saloon.
Officers and crew: 320.
Maiden voyage: Bremen—Southampton—Cher-
  bourg—New York on August 5, 1927.

Launched as *Zeppelin* in June 1914, but comple-
tion was suspended until after the war. Partially
completed in 1919 and surrendered to the United
States on April 4, 1919, for five trips repatriating
American troops back home. Allotted to the British
Shipping Controller in November 1919 and man-
aged by the White Star Line. Sold to the Orient
Line in 1920 and completed as the *Ormuz*. Resold
to the North German Lloyd in 1927 and renamed
Dresden. She was originally built for the Australian

trade, but was used in the Bremen—Boulogne—
Cobh—New York service and later on cruising
extensively. Struck a rock in the Bokn Fjord near
Kopervik, Norway, on June 20, 1934, while on a
North Sea cruise with about one thousand passengers on board. The *Dresden* was beached on the
island of Karmoy, but became a total loss and sank
the next day. Four lives were lost in the launching
of the lifeboats.

II EUROPA

Builder: Blohm & Voss, Hamburg, Germany.
Completed: March 1930.
Gross tonnage: 49746.
Dimensions: 936ft × 102ft. Depth 48ft.
Engines: Twelve steam turbines, single-reduction geared.
Screws: Quadruple.
Watertight bulkheads: Fourteen.
Decks: Seven.
Normal speed: 27.50 knots.
Passenger accommodation: 723 first, 616 tourist, and 905 third class.
Maiden voyage: Bremen–Southampton–Cherbourg–New York on March 19, 1930.

She was launched on August 15, 1928, but her maiden voyage was held up due to a fire on board while being fitted out on March 26, 1929. Won the Blue Riband from her sister *Bremen* in 1930 by making the run from Cherbourg to Ambrose Lighthouse in 4 days, 17 hours, and 6 minutes at a speed of 27.91 knots. A fast ship, but not as able as the *Bremen*, she soon lost the position. *Europa* also carried a catapult like the *Bremen* for launching a seaplane to expedite the mail. Served in the Bremen–Channel ports–New York service until the outbreak of war in September 1939. She was then moved to Hamburg and later used as a naval accommodation ship at Keil, Germany, for a time. Sold to the German-American Line in 1941 and commissioned by the United States after the war for repatriating troops. Allotted to France in May 1946 and transferred to the French Line in July 1946 who renamed her *Liberte*. Sold to Italian shipbreakers on December 30, 1961.
Sister ship: *Bremen*.

III EUROPA

Builder: De Schelde N.V., Flushing, Netherlands.
Completed: October 1953.
Gross tonnage: 21514.
Dimensions: 600ft × 77ft. Depth 49ft.
Engines: Two Burmeister & Wain eight-
cylinder, two-stroke, single-acting diesel.
Screws: Twin.
Collision bulkhead: One.
Watertight bulkheads: Eight.
Decks: Five.
Normal speed: 17.50 knots.
Officers and crew: 418.
Passenger accommodation: 176 first and 630
tourist class. (Accommodations are reduced to
400 in a single class when in cruise service.)
Maiden voyage: Bremerhaven–Southampton–
Cherbourg–New York on January 9, 1966.

Built for the Swedish-American Line and christened *Kungsholm*. Sold to the North German Lloyd in October 1965 and renamed *Europa*. Engaged in the Bremerhaven–Southampton–Cherbourg–New York run with cruises during the off-seasonal months to the West Indies and special cruises. A most beautiful liner designed with many old-world ideas and comforts with such modern conveniences as air-conditioning and Denny-Brown stabilisers. All cabins are situated outside and her fore-funnel is a dummy. She has a fuel capacity of some 1712 metric tons and a daily consumption of 55 metric tons. The *Europa* commenced a number of cruises from Bremerhaven and Genoa between April 25 and August 25 of 1971. On September 1, 1970, she passed on to Hapag-Lloyd ownership with both companies holding an equal percentage of the preferred stock. Hapag is known as the Hamburg-America Line and the Lloyd has been substituted for North German Lloyd. Presently in service. It should be noted that the name North German Lloyd is still used in relation to the *Europa*.

FRIEDRICH DER GROSSE

Builder: A.G. Vulkan, Stettin, Germany.
Completed: November 1896.
Gross tonnage: 10771.
Dimensions: 546ft × 60ft. Depth 35ft.
Engines: Two four-cylinder, quadruple
   expansion.
Screws: Twin.
Watertight bulkheads: Twelve.
Decks: Four.
Normal speed: 15 knots.
Passenger accommodation: 226 first, 235
   second and 1671 steerage.
Officers and crew: 222.
Maiden voyage: Bremen—Australia in November
   1896.

Employed in the Bremen—Southampton—New York run in the summer and in the Bremen—Southampton—via Suez Canal—Adelaide—Melbourne — Sydney trade during the winter months. The *Friedrich der Grosse* made her last voyage to Australia on January 18, 1914, and was later seized by the United States Government in April 1917 while she had been interned at the port of New York since the outbreak of war. Commissioned as a transport and renamed *Huron*. Sold to the Los Angeles Steamship Co in 1922 and renamed *City of Honolulu*. Caught fire on her return maiden voyage from Honolulu to San Pedro on October 12, 1922, and was sunk by gunfire from the US Army transport *Thomas* after evacuating her passengers and crew.
Sister ship: *Konigin Luise.*

GEORGE WASHINGTON

Builder: A.G. Vulkan, Stettin, Germany
Completed: June 1909.
Gross tonnage: 25570.
Dimensions: 723ft×78ft. Depth 50ft.
Engines: Two four-cylinder, quadruple expansion.
Screws: Twin.
Watertight bulkheads: Twelve.
Decks: Six.
Normal speed: 19 knots.
Passenger accommodation: 568 first, 433 second and 1226 steerage.
Maiden voyage: Bremen—Southampton—Cherbourg—New York on June 12, 1909.

The *George Washington* had a promenade deck 328ft long. Employed in the Bremen—Southampton—Cherbourg—New York run with a call at Plymouth eastbound in place of Southampton. In 1913 Mr Ferencz Vaszily purchased the ten-millionth ticket from the North German Lloyd on the *George Washington* and was given a special accommodation by the Line. Interned at New York on June 9, 1914, and seized by the United States on April 4, 1917. She was converted to a transport without a change in name. In 1919 she was used to carry President Wilson and his staff to the Versailles Peace Conferences. Turned over to the United States Shipping Board in 1919 and managed by the United States Mail Line from August 1920 until August 31, 1921, when the company went bankrupt and she was released to the newly born US Lines. Taken over by the British in 1940 and renamed *Catlin* in 1941 after having been laid up since September 1932 and converted to a transport. Returned to the United States the following year and recovered her own name. Sold for scrap in January 1951 after having been destroyed by fire at Baltimore on January 16.

GNEISENAU

Builder: Deutsche Schiff-und-Maschinenbau,
  AG Weser, Bremen, Germany.
Completed: 1935.
Gross tonnage: 18160.
Dimensions: 652ft × 74ft. Depth 45ft.
Engines: Two sets of steam turbines.
Screws: Twin.
Decks: Four.
Normal speed: 20 knots.
Passenger accommodation: 186 first and 150
  tourist class.

Employed in the Bremen–Genoa–via Suez Canal–
Shanghai service. She and her sister *Scharnhorst*
are the largest ships to date with a maierform bow
and are classified as cargo-passenger liners with a
cargo capacity of 10800 tons. Used for troop work
by the Nazis during World War II and sunk by a
mine in the Baltic Sea while *en route* to Russia
with troops on May 21, 1943. The *Gneisenau* was
beached on the island of Lloland, Denmark,
where she lay on her side half submerged.
Broken up by Danish shipbreakers after the war.
Sister ships: *Potsdam* and *Scharnhorst*.

GROSSER KURFURST

Builder: F. Schichau, Danzig, Germany.
Completed: April 1900.
Gross tonnage: 13102.
Dimensions: 580ft × 62ft. Depth 36ft.
Engines: Two four-cylinder, quadruple
  expansion.
Screws: Twin.
Watertight bulkheads: Twelve.
Decks: Four.
Normal speed: 16 knots.
Passenger accommodation: 434 first, 176
  second and 1211 steerage.
Officers and crew: 273.
Maiden voyage: Bremen—New York on May 5,
  1900.

Engaged in the alternate services from Bremen to New York and Central America and from Bremen to Southampton, Suez Canal, Albany, Adelaide, Melbourne and Sydney making her last such voyage on January 21, 1912. On October 9, 1913, she rescued 105 persons from the Royal Line emigrant ship *Volturno*, ablaze in the Atlantic. The *Grosser Kurfurst* had played a major part in the life-saving operations, having rescued the greater number of people in comparison with the eight other assisting vessels. Interned at New York in 1914 and seized by the United States in April 1917. She was converted to a transport under the name of *Aeolus*. Sold to the Munson Line in 1921 and subsequently to the Los Angeles Steamship Co in 1922 who renamed her *City of Los Angeles*. Sold to Japanese shipbreakers in April 1937.

II KAISER WILHELM II

Builder: A.G. Vulkan, Stettin, Germany.
Completed: March 1903.
Gross tonnage: 19361.
Dimensions: 707ft × 72ft. Depth 52ft.
Engines: Four four-cylinder, quadruple expansion.
Screws: Twin.
Watertight bulkheads: Sixteen.
Decks: Six.
Normal speed: 22.75 knots.
Officers and crew: 600.
Passenger accommodation: 646 first, 346 second and 799 third class.
Maiden voyage: Bremen–Southampton–Cherbourg–New York on April 14, 1903.
Last voyage for North German Lloyd Line: Bremen–Cherbourg–New York on July 14, 1914.

Her coal bunkers held 5625 tons of coal and she consumed 700 tons of it within a 24-hour period. The *Kaiser Wilhelm II* was the largest merchant liner to date when constructed. Won the Blue Riband from the *Kronprinz Wilhelm* in September 1904 by making the run from Sandy Hook to Plymouth in 5 days, 8 hours, and 20 minutes at a speed of 23.30 knots. Employed in the Bremen–Southampton–Cherbourg–New York service with calls at Plymouth eastbound. Interned at New York Harbour on June 24, 1914, and seized by the United States on April 6, 1917, and renamed *Agamemnon* for use as a transport. Transferred to the United States Mail Line by the United States Shipping Board in 1920, but never sailed again. Laid up in the Chesapeake Bay and renamed *Monticello* in 1927. Offered to Britain in 1940, but was declined and sold for scrap at Baltimore for the sum of $183500.
Sister ship: *Kronprinzessin Cecilie.*

KAISER WILHELM DER GROSSE

Builder A.G. Vulkan, Stettin, Germany.
Completed: September 1897.
Gross tonnage: 14349.
Dimensions: 649ft × 66ft. Depth 43ft.
Engines: Two four-cylinder, quadruple expansion.
Screws: Twin.
Watertight bulkheads: Fourteen.
Decks: Four.
Normal speed: 22.50 knots.
Officers and crew: 492.
Passenger accommodation: 332 first, 343 second, and 1074 third class.
Maiden voyage: Bremen–Southampton–New York on September 19, 1897.

Won the Blue Riband from the Cunard Line's *Lucania* on her maiden voyage by making the run from the Needles to Sandy Hook in 5 days, 22 hours and 45 minutes at a speed of 21.39 knots. Engaged in the Bremen–Southampton–Cherbourg–New York run with a call at Plymouth eastbound in place of Southampton. The *Kaiser Wilhelm der Grosse* was the first liner to ever win the Blue Riband for the Line and the first ship to be ever built with four stacks. She was also the first to carry a wireless radio which was installed in February 1900 with a power radius of 25 miles. Another of her first-to-carry innovations were her remote control watertight doors. On June 30, 1900, the *Kaiser Wilhelm* was present at the great dock fire at Hoboken, New Jersey, but was towed away from the blazing wharfs without being damaged. To maintain her high speed her stokeholds consumed 528 tons of coal every 24 hours. Made her last transatlantic voyage on November 11, 1913, from New York to Plymouth, Cherbourg and Bremen and was fitted out as an armed commerce raider. On August 28, 1914, she was after a short career as a raider damaged by gunfire from the British cruiser *Highflyer* at Rio de Oro, Africa, while taking on bunkers. The crew, anticipating inevitable surrender, scuttled the ship and escaped to the Hamburg-America store's ship *Bethania* which chanced to be alongside of her.
Sister ship: *Kronprinz Wilhelm.*

KONIG ALBERT

Builder: A.G. Vulkan, Stettin, Germany.
Completed: September 1899.
Gross tonnage: 10484.
Dimensions: 499ft × 60ft. Depth 35ft.
Engines: Two four-cylinder, quadruple expansion.
Screws: Twin.
Decks: Four.
Normal speed: 15 knots.
Passenger accommodation: 227 first, 119 second and 1799 steerage.
Officers and crew: 230.
Maiden voyage: Bremen—Yokohama on October 4, 1899.
Last voyage for North German Lloyd Line: New York—Naples on July 4, 1914.

Engaged in the Bremen—Eastern Asia service until she was diverted to the Bremen—Cherbourg—New York run on March 13, 1903. Reallocated to the Naples—New York service in 1905. Seized by the Italian Government in June 1915 for use as a hospital ship and renamed *Ferdinando Palasciano* in 1917. Transferrred to the Italian Navy in 1924 and sold for scrap in Italy in 1926.

KONIGIN LUISE

Builder: A.G. Vulkan, Stettin, Germany.
Completed: March 1897.
Gross tonnage: 10785.
Dimensions: 544ft × 60ft. Depth 35ft.
Engines: Two four-cylinder, quadruple
   expansion.
Screws: Twin.
Watertight bulkheads: Twelve.
Decks: Four.
Normal speed: 15.50 knots.
Passenger accommodation: 227 first, 235
   second and 1564 steerage.
Officers and crew: 231.
Maiden voyage: Bremen—New York on March 22,
   1897.
Last voyage for North German Lloyd Line: Balti-
   more—Bremen on July 15, 1914.

Engaged in the Bremen—Southampton—New York service in the summer and from Bremen to Southampton, Suez Canal, Adelaide, Melbourne and Sydney during the winter months. Re-allocated to the Naples—New York run from 1904 until sometime in 1910 when she reverted back to her original services and commenced her last voyage to Australia on October 29, 1911, from Bremen to Southampton, Suez Canal, Adelaide,

Melbourne and Sydney. Allotted to the British in 1919 as a World War I reparation and sold by the British Shipping Controller to the Orient Line the following year and renamed *Omar*. Resold to the Byron Steamship Co in 1924 and renamed *Edison*. Passed on to the ownership of the National Steam Navigation Co of Greece in 1929 and retained her name. Sold to Italian shipbreakers in July 1935.
Sister ship: *Friedrich der Grosse*

KRONPRINZESSIN CECILIE

Builder: A.G. Vulkan, Stettin, Germany.
Completed: July 1907.
Gross tonnage: 19503.
Dimensions: 706ft × 72ft. Depth 52ft.
Engines: Four four-cylinder, quadruple expansion.
Screws: Twin.
Watertight bulkheads: Sixteen.
Decks: Six.
Normal speed: 22.75 knots.
Passenger accommodation: 617 first, 326 second and 798 third class.
Maiden voyage: Bremen–Southampton–Cherbourg–New York on August 6, 1907.
Last commercial voyage for North German Lloyd Line: Bremen–Cherbourg on July 14, 1914.
Officers and crew: 602.

Engaged in the Bremen–Southampton–Cherbourg–New York run with calls at Plymouth eastbound. When World War I broke out in August 1914 the *Kronprinzessin* chanced to be at sea eastbound with a passenger clientage worth many millions of dollars. In consideration for the passengers and their safety, from the British raiders which would be prowling the North Atlantic waters, the captain ordered that the funnels be painted black at their tops, so as to appear to be the White Star liner *Olympic*, and headed back to American waters. On the morning of August 4, 1914, she anchored at Bar Harbour, Maine, and word had spread that the *Olympic* was in the harbour. The incident gave birth to her being known as 'The Kaiser's Treasure Ship' because of the amount of specie aboard and her elusive tactics of camouflage. Seized by the United States for troop service on April 6, 1917, at Boston where she had been interned since August 1914 and renamed *Mount Vernon* for troop work. Torpedoed on September 5, 1918, off Brest, France, but managed to make port with a list of 15 degrees and a drop in her speed of six knots. Thirty-six lives were lost when the bulkheads of the engine room were closed after she was hit. Transferred to the United States Mail Line in 1920, but never sailed again. She was vainly offered to Britain in 1940 and refused after she had laid in the Chesapeake Bay for 20 years. Sold for scrap at Baltimore for $178300 by the United States Shipping Board in July 1940.
Sister ship: *Kaiser Wilhelm II*.

KRONPRINZ WILHELM

Builder: A.G. Vulkan, Stettin, Germany.
Completed: August 1901.
Gross tonnage: 14908.
Dimensions: 663ft × 66ft. Depth 43ft.
Engines: Two six-cylinder, quadruple expansion.
Screws: Twin.
Watertight bulkhead: Ten.
Decks: Four.
Normal speed: 22.75 knots. (Attained a speed of 23.34 knots on her trials.)
Passenger accommodation: 593 first, 362 second and 696 third class.
Officers and crew: 527.
Maiden voyage: Bremen—Southampton—Cherbourg—New York on September 17, 1901.
Last voyage for North German Lloyd Line: Bremen—Cherbourg—New York on July 21, 1914.

Won the Blue Riband from the Hamburg-America Line's *Deutschland* in September 1902 by making the run from Cherbourg to Sandy Hook in 5 days, 11 hours and 57 minutes at a speed of 23.09 knots. Employed in the Bremen—Southampton—Cherbourg—New York run with a call at Plymouth in place of Southampton homeward. The *Kronprinz Wilhelm* was fitted out as an armed commerce raider during World War I and began her career on July 22, 1914, when she left New York for the West Indies escorted by the German cruiser *Karlsruhe*. On April 10, 1915, she arrived at Chesapeake Bay only to be greeted by a blockade of British cruisers. Awaiting for night to fall, the *Kronprinz* made a last desperate run to break through. Her stokers fed the fires with such labour that the *Kronprinz* began to tremble, but up went the pressure gauges producing speed that never seemed possible. She broke through the array of cruisers before they had a chance to set their guns on her and made it to safety, but had burst her lungs in the process. Seized by the United States at Norfolk, Virginia, in April 1917 for troop service and renamed *Von Steuben*. Sold for scrap in 1923 after having been completely worn out by the war and laying in reserve. During her career as a German commerce raider the *Kronprinz Wilhelm* sank 26 vessels totalling over 58000 tons gross and steamed over 37000 miles mostly in the South Atlantic.
Sister ship: *Kaiser Wilhelm der Grosse.*

II MAIN

Builder: Blohm & Voss, Hamburg, Germany.
Completed: April 1900.
Gross tonnage: 10058.
Dimensions: 520ft × 58ft. Depth 37ft.
Engines: Two four-cylinder, quadruple
  expansion.
Screws: Twin.
Normal speed: 13.50 knots.
Passenger accommodation: 511 second and 2887
  third class.
Officers and crew: 174.
Maiden voyage: Bremen—New York—Baltimore on
  April 28, 1900.
Last voyage for North German Lloyd Line: Balti-
  more—Bremen on July 8, 1914.

Employed in the Bremen—Baltimore—New York service. The *Main* was present at the great dock fire at Hoboken, New Jersey, on June 30, 1900, and was damaged to some extent. Laid up at Antwerp, Belgium, between 1914—18 and allo-cated to Britain in 1919 as a World War I repara-tion. She was soon transferred to France under the same circumstances in 1920 and scrapped in 1925 in France.
Sister ships: *Neckar* and *Rhein*

III MÜNCHEN

Builder: Vulkan Werkes, Stettin, Germany.
Completed: May 1923.
Gross tonnage: 14660.
Dimensions: 551ft × 65ft. Depth 35ft.
Engines: Two four-cylinder, triple-expansion engines and low-pressure turbines.
Screws: Twin.
Watertight bulkheads: Twelve.
Decks: Four.
Normal speed: 16 knots.
Passenger accommodation: 214 cabin, 358 tourist, and 221 third class.
Officers and crew: 356.
Maiden voyage: Bremen—New York on June 21, 1923.

Engaged in the Bremen—Southampton—Cherbourg—New York service with a call at Plymouth eastbound instead of Southampton. Damaged by fire at New York in 1930 and taken back to Bremen to be rebuilt. She emerged with a totally different profile by the elimination of a funnel; a maierform bow; conversion to oil fuel and renamed *General von Steuben* in 1931 when completed. In 1933 she was used exclusively as the Line's cruise ship, but made several voyages to New York in the years following. Her name was later contracted to *Steuben* in 1939 when the Nazi Government had hinted that the General after whom she was named left the Prussian Army for allegiance to another country. Sunk by a Russian submarine off Stolpmunde, Germany, on February 10, 1945, with an estimated loss of 3,000 of the 4,000 East Prussian immigrants that she was transporting to Germany.
Sister ship: *Stuttgart.*

POTSDAM

Builder: Blohm & Voss, KaA Hamburg, Germany.
Completed: June 1935.
Gross tonnage: 17528.
Dimensions: 634ft × 74ft. Depth 45ft.
Engines: Steam turbines connected to electric motors.
Screws: Twin.
Watertight bulkheads: Eleven.
Decks: Four.
Normal speed: 20 knots.
Passenger accommodation: 227 first and 166 tourist class.
Officers and crew: 275.
Maiden voyage: Bremerhaven—Southampton—East Asia on July 5, 1935.

Engaged in the Bremen—Genoa—Shanghai trade. Captured by the allies in 1945 and allotted to the British Ministry of Transport in 1946 and renamed *Empire Fowey*. Refitted in 1946 and resumed services in 1950 being managed by the

P & O Line during the period following the war. Sold to the Pan-Islamic Steamship Co in May 1960 and renamed *Safina-E-Hujjaj*.
(See Notes on p. 223.)
Sister ships: *Gneisenau* and *Scharnhorst.*

PRINZESS ALICE

Builder: A.G. Vulkan, Stettin, Germany
Completed: December 1900.
Gross tonnage: 10981.
Dimensions: 523ft × 60ft. Depth 38ft.
Engines: Two four-cylinder, quadruple
   expansion.
Screws: Twin.
Watertight bulkheads: Thirteen.
Decks: Four.
Normal speed: 15.50 knots.
Passenger accommodation: 199 first, 300 second,
   and 1863 third class.
Officers and crew: 230.

Built for the Hamburg-America Line and christened *Kiautschou*. Sold to the North German Lloyd in 1903 and renamed *Prinzess Alice*. Engaged in the Bremen–Far Eastern trade, but made some voyages to New York. Seized in 1917 by the United States at Manila, Philippines, and renamed *Princess Matoika* for transport work. Transferred to the United States Mail Line in 1921 and made five voyages until taken over by the United States Line in August 1921 and renamed *President Arthur* in 1922. Sold to the Palace Line in 1924 and renamed *White Palace*. Resold to the Los Angeles Steamship Co in 1928 and renamed *City of Honolulu*. Damaged by fire on May 25, 1930 at Honolulu, she made the trip back to Los Angeles and was laid up until sold to Japanese shipbreakers in 1933.

PRINZESS IRENE

Builder: A.G. Vulkan, Stettin, Germany.
Completed: September 1900.
Gross tonnage: 10893.
Dimensions: 523ft × 60ft. Depth 38ft.
Engines: Two four-cylinder, quadruple expansion.
Screws: Twin.
Watertight bulkheads: Thirteen.
Decks: Four.
Normal speed: 15.50 knots.
Passenger accommodation; 217 first, 350 second, and 1954 third class.
Maiden voyage: Bremen–Southampton–via Suez Canal–China–Japan on November 3, 1900.
Officers and crew: 230.

Engaged in the Bremen–Southampton–Far Eastern trade, but was reallocated to the Bremen–Southampton–New York run on March 27, 1903. Transferred to the Mediterranean trade to New York in April 1903 and made some voyages from Hamburg to New York. Laid up at New York in 1914 and seized by the United States in April 1917 and renamed *Pocahontas* for transport work. Transferred to the United States Mail Line in 1921 and made three trips. Returned to the United States Shipping Board and offered for repurchase to the North German Lloyd in early 1923. Repurchased and acquired the name of *Bremen*, now being the third vessel to carry the name and resumed services for the Line in April 1923 from Bremen to New York. In 1928 she was renamed *Karlsruhe* with the building of a fourth *Bremen*. Sold for scrap in Germany in July 1933.
Sister ship: *Prinzess Alice*.

PRINZ FRIEDRICH WILHELM

Builder: J. C. Tecklenborg, A.G. Geestmunde.
  Germany.
Completed: May 1908.
Gross tonnage: 17082.
Dimensions: 613ft × 68ft. Depth 39ft.
Engines: Two four-cylinder, quadruple
  expansion.
Screws: Twin.
Watertight bulkheads: Ten.
Decks: Four.
Normal speed: 17 knots.
Passenger accommodation: 365 first, 372 sec-
  ond, and 1741 third class.
Officers and crew: 401
Maiden voyage: Bremen–New York on June 6,
  1908.

Placed in the Bremen–Southampton–Cherbourg–
New York service with a call at Plymouth east-
bound in place of Southampton on April 2, 1910.
She had been previously in another service of the
Line before being placed in the North Atlantic
run. She had been an extra service liner of the
company. Commenced her last voyage for the
North German Lloyd's North Atlantic service on
June 27, 1914, from New York to Plymouth,
Cherbourg and Bremen. Allotted to the British
Shipping Controller in 1919 after she was used by
the United States Navy for a period. Chartered to
the Canadian-Pacific in 1920. Purchased by
them in 1922 and renamed *Empress of India:
Montlaurier* in 1922; *Monteith* in 1925; and
lastly *Montnairn* in 1925. Sold to shipbreakers in
1929 and scrapped by March 1930.
Sister ship: *Berlin*.

II RHEIN

Builder: Blohm & Voss, Hamburg, Germany.
Completed: December 1899.
Gross tonnage: 10058.
Dimensions: 520ft × 58ft. Depth 37ft.
Engines: Two four-cylinder, quadruple expansion.
Screws: Twin.
Watertight bulkheads: Eleven.
Decks: Four.
Normal speed: 13.50 knots.
Passenger accommodation: 486 second and 2495 third class.
Officers and crew: 174.
Maiden voyage: Bremen—New York on December 9, 1899.

Engaged in the Bremen—Baltimore—New York service in the summer and from Bremen to Southampton, Suez Canal, Albany, Adelaide, Melbourne and Sydney. Completed her last such voyage on November 27, 1904, and was settled in the North Atlantic services. Seized by the United States at Baltimore on April 6, 1917 and renamed *Susquehanna* for use as a transport. Managed by the United States Mail Line in August 1930 and later passed on to United States Lines ownership the following August 31. Tonnage was now 9959 and she made her last voyage in August 1922 and was subsequently laid up. Sold to Japanese shipbreakers in November 1928.
Sister ships: *Main* and *Neckar*.

II SCHARNHORST

Builder: Deutsche Schiff-und-Maschinenbau,
AG Weser, Flensburg, Germany.
Completed: April 1935.
Gross tonnage: 18184.
Dimensions: 652ft × 74ft. Depth 45ft.
Engines: Two steam turbines connected to two
electric motors.
Screws: Twin.
Decks: Four.
Normal speed: 20 knots. (Attained a speed of 21
knots during her trials.)
Passenger accommodation: 186 first and 150
tourist class.
Officers and crew: 281
Maiden voyage: Bremerhaven—Far East on May 3,
1935.

Engaged in the Bremen—Southampton—Genoa—via Suez Canal—Shanghai trade. She and her sister *Gneisenau* are the largest ships to date with a maier-form bow and are classified as cargo-passenger liners with a cargo capacity of 10800 tons. Laid up in Japan in September 1939 and sold to the Japanese on July 2, 1942. Renamed *Jinyo* after conversion to an escort aircraft in December 1943. Sunk by the U.S. submarine *Spadefish* 140 miles northeast of Shanghai on November 17, 1944.

II SIERRA CORDOBA

Builder: Bremer Vulkan, Vegesack, Germany.
Completed: January 1924.
Gross tonnage: 11492.
Dimensions: 511ft × 66ft. Depth 34ft.
Engines: Two three-cylinder triple expansion.
Screws: Twin.
Watertight bulkheads: Nine.
Decks: Four.
Normal speed: 14.50 knots.
Passenger accommodation: 150 first, 270
    second and 890 third class.
Officers and crew: 300.
Maiden voyage: Bremerhaven—River Plate, South
    America, on January 26, 1924.

Engaged in the Bremen—South American trade.
Appropriated by the Nazi German Labour Ministry
in 1935, but remained under the North German
Lloyd's management. Sold for scrap in 1948.
Sister ships: *Sierra Morena* and *Sierra Ventana*.

SIERRA MORENA

Builder: Bremer Vulkan, Vegesack, Germany.
Completed: October 1924.
Gross tonnage: 11430.
Dimensions: 511ft × 66ft. Depth 34ft.
Engines: Two three-cylinder, triple expansion.
Screws: Twin.
Watertight bulkheads: Nine.
Decks: Four.
Normal speed: 14.50 knots.
Passenger accommodation: 150 first, 270 second and 890 third class.
Officers and crew: 298.
Maiden voyage: Bremerhaven—River Plate, South America, on October 25, 1924.

Employed in the Bremen—South American trade. Renamed *Der Deutsche* in 1934 and appropriated by the Nazi German Labour Ministry in 1935, but remained under North German Lloyd management. She now carried her complement of 1000 passengers in a single cabin-class. Ceded to the Russians in June 1946 as a World War II reparation and renamed *Asia*. She re-entered services for them in 1950 after being refitted by the Warnow Werft yards in East Germany. Scrapped in Russia in 1970.
Sister ships: *Sierra Cordoba* and *Sierra Ventana*.

II SIERRA VENTANA

Builder: Bremer Vulkan, Vegesack, Germany.
Completed: August 1923.
Gross tonnage: 11392.
Dimensions: 511ft×66ft. Depth 34ft.
Engines: Two three-cylinder, triple expansion.
Screws: Twin.
Watertight bulkheads: Nine.
Decks: Four.
Normal speed: 14.50 knots.
Passenger accommodation: 692 cabin and 540
    third class.
Officers and crew: 264.
Maiden voyage: Bremerhaven—New York on Sep-
    tember 8, 1924.

Employed in the Bremen—South American trade,
but made some voyages to New York in 1923.
Sold to the Italian Line in 1935 and renamed
Sardegna. Resold to the Lloyd Triestino in 1937
and sunk by an allied submarine on December 29,
1940.
Sister ships: *Sierra Cordoba* and *Sierra Morena*.

II STUTTGART

Builder: Vulkan Werkes, Stettin, Germany.
Completed: January 1924.
Gross tonnage: 13387.
Dimensions: 551ft × 65ft. Depth 35ft.
Engines: Two three-cylinder, triple expansion.
Screws: Twin.
Watertight bulkheads: Twelve.
Decks: Four.
Normal speed: 16 knots.
Passenger accommodation: 171 first, 421 second, and 594 third class.
Officers and crew: 356.
Maiden voyage: Bremerhaven—New York on January 15, 1924.

Employed in the Bremen—New York service and was later placed in the Far Eastern trade in 1930. Appropriated by the Nazi German Labour Ministry in 1938, but remained under the management of the North German Lloyd. Burnt out and completely destroyed by an allied air attack on Gdynia, Poland, on October 9, 1943.
Sister ship: *München*.

NORWEGIAN-AMERICA LINE

I BERGENSFJORD

Builder: Cammell, Laird & Co Ltd, Birkenhead, England.
Completed: September 1913.
Gross tonnage: 11015.
Dimensions: 530ft × 61ft. Depth 33ft.
Engines: Two four-cylinder, quadruple expansion engines and two low-pressure turbines, double-reduction, geared.
Screws: Twin.
Watertight bulkheads: Eight.
Decks: Three.
Normal speed: 15 knots.
Passenger accommodation: 1000 in first, second and third classes.
Maiden voyage: Kristiania—Bergen—New York, arriving on October 7, 1913.

Engaged in the Oslo—Copenhagen—Bergen—New York service year-round. The *Bergensfjord* maintained regular sailings between Bergen and New York throughout World War I. She was formerly driven by only reciprocating machinery until early 1932 when the two low-pressure turbines were added. On April 15, 1940, she arrived at New York and was laid up until November 1941 when she sailed to Halifax to be converted to a transport.

Laid up after World War II. She was sold to the Home Lines in November 1946 and renamed *Argentina* after having served the Norwegian—America Line for three long decades. Resold to the Zim Lines in 1952 and renamed *Jerusalem: Aliya* in 1957. Sold to the Terrestse Marittima for scrapping at Spezia, Italy, in October 1959.
Sister ship: *Kristianiafjord.*

II BERGENSFJORD

Builder: Swan, Hunter & Wigham Richardson, Ltd.,
 Wallsend-on-Tyne, England.
Completed: May 1956.
Gross Tonnage: 18739.
Dimensions: 578ft × 72ft. Depth 47ft.
Engines: Two eight-cylinder, two-stroke, double-act-
 ing diesel.
Screws: Twin.
Decks: Five.
Normal speed: 20 knots.
Passenger accommodation: 103 first and 774
 tourist class.
Maiden voyage: Oslo—Bergen—New York on May
 30, 1956.

Engaged in the Oslo—Copenhagen—Kristiansand—New York run with a call at Stavanger instead of Kristiansand during the summer season and cruising from Port Everglades to the West Indies during some of the off-seasonal months. On October 20, 1970, she made a 59-day cruise from New York calling at sixteen ports in the Pacific. Sold to the French Line in March 1971, and renamed *De Grasse.* Resold to the Thorensen Co. of Singapore in 1973 and renamed *Rasa Sa Yang.* Presently in their service.

KRISTIANIAFJORD

Builder: Cammell, Laird & Co Ltd, Birkenhead, England.
Completed: May 1913.
Gross tonnage: 10669.
Dimensions: 530ft × 61ft. Depth 33ft.
Engines: Two four-cylinder, quadruple expansion engines and two low-pressure turbines, double-reduction geared.

Screws: Twin.
Watertight bulkheads: Eight.
Decks: Three.
Normal speed: 15 knots.
Passenger accommodation: 165 first, 235 second, and 907 third class.
Maiden voyage: Kristiania—Bergen—New York on June 4, 1913.
Last voyage: From New York on July 7, 1917.

Engaged in the Oslo—Copenhagen—Bergen—New York service. The *Kristianiafjord* made two trips to America without passengers after United States' entry into the war in April 1917. Wrecked seven miles off Cape Race, Newfoundland, on July 15, 1917.
Sister ship: *Bergensfjord.*

I OSLOFJORD

Builder: Deutsche Schiff-und-Maschinenbau, AG Weser, Bremen, Germany.
Completed: June 1938.
Gross tonnage: 18673.
Dimensions: 588ft × 73ft. Depth 43ft.
Engines: Four seven-cylinder, two-stroke, double-acting diesel.
Screws: Twin.
Normal speed: 18 knots.
Maiden voyage: Oslo–Bergen–New York on June 4, 1938.
Passenger accommodation: 152 cabin, 307 tourist, and 401 third class.

Engaged in the Oslo–Scandinavian ports–New York run until she was laid up at the Bayonne terminal at New York in the spring of 1940. On October 26, 1940, she was taken to Halifax and fitted out as a transport and completed by November. Sunk by an acoustic mine near the mouth of the Tyne River, England, on December 13, 1940, while *en route* to join the British Ministry of Transport Fleet. All of her 240 crew members were saved except one and the ship was beached, but became a total loss. An extremely short life for a liner and a great loss to the Norwegian-America Line.

II OSLOFJORD

Builder: Netherlands Dock & Engineering Co, Amsterdam, Netherlands.
Completed: November 1949.
Gross tonnage: 16923.
Dimensions: 577ft×72ft. Depth 38ft.
Engines: Two seven-cylinder, two-stroke, double-acting Stork diesel.
Screws: Twin.
Decks: Five.
Normal speed: 20 knots. (Attained a speed of 21.74 knots on her trial runs.)
Passenger accommodation: 266 first and 359 tourist class.
Maiden voyage: Oslo–Copenhagen–Kristiansand–Stavanger–Bergen–New York on November 26, 1949.

Employed in the Oslo–Scandinavian ports–New York run and cruising. Fitted with motion stabilisers in November 1957. In 1969 she was chartered to the Coast Lines for a three-year term and was renamed *Fulvia*. On July 19, 1970, when a hundred miles north of the Canary Islands she was engulfed by flames from stem to stern due to an explosion in the engine room. The fire was so intense that her funnel melted as if it were a mass of plastic. At the time she was on a cruise with 721 passengers and crew on board who were all safely disembarked by lifeboats and the assisting French ship *Acnerville*. The ship's last moments were recorded as listing heavily to port before she plunged to the depths at 11.45am on the 20th, 36 hours after the explosion. The *Oslofjord* was lost by fire, which has taken many ships to their end, but this time in the hands of strangers.

SAGAFJORD

Builder: Societe des Forges et Chantiers de la Mediterranee, Le Seyne, France.
Completed: September 1965.
Gross tonnage: 24002.
Dimensions: 620ft × 80ft. Depth 55ft.
Engines: Two nine-cylinder, two-cycle, single-acting Sulzer diesel.
Screws: Twin.
Decks: Five.
Normal speed: 20 knots. (Attained a speed of over 22.50 knots during her trials.)
Passenger accommodation: 70 first and 719 tourist class. (Accommodations are limited to 450 when pleasure-cruising.)
Maiden voyage: Oslo–Kristiansand–Copenhagen–New York on October 2, 1965.

The *Sagafjord*'s superstructure is constructed of aluminium. She is furnished with two electrically operated bow thrusters athwartship, plus six Bergen diesel locomotive-type auxiliary engines, which latter are the first to be used on a ship. Equipped with Denny-Brown motion stabilisers and fully air-conditioned. The *Sagafjord* is the Norwegian-America Line's flagship. Employed in the Oslo–Copenhagen–Kristiansand–New York service with a call at Stavanger instead of Kristiansand during the summer months. She has since her entry into service been used mostly as a cruise ship all-year-round with only a few trans-atlantic voyages. On January 5, 1971, she made a 93-day cruise from New York calling at 29 ports in the Pacific and makes this same cruise every year. Presently in service.

STAVANGERFJORD

Builder: Cammell, Laird & Co Ltd, Birkenhead, England.
Completed: February 1918.
Gross tonnage: 14015.
Dimensions: 553ft × 64ft. Depth 33ft.
Engines: Two four-cylinder, quadruple expansion engines and two low-pressure turbines, double reduction geared.
Screws: Twin.
Watertight bulkheads: Ten.
Decks: Four.
Normal speed: 15.50 knots.
Passenger accommodation: 90 first, 172 cabin and 413 tourist class.
Maiden voyage: Kristiania—Bergen—New York on April 29, 1918.

The *Stavangerfjord* was built to replace the loss of the *Kristianiafjord* and was employed in the Oslo—Copenhagen—New York run. Refitted for oil fuel in March 1924 and two low-pressure turbines added to her reciprocating machinery in late 1931. In April 1940 she was commandeered by the Germans and used as an hotel-ship to accommodate troops. Returned back to the Line after World War II and resumed transatlantic sailings in August 1945 first as a repatriation ship and subsequently on commercial services. On December 9, 1953, the *Stavangerfjord* lost her rudder in a gale 500 miles east of Newfoundland and hove to for two days until the Norwegian-America Line's freighter *Lyngenfjord* took the ship in tow. While in tow the lines broke, but she was able to make Oslo on her own by the 19th. Reconditioned in November—December 1956. *Stavangerfjord* was the oldest known passenger ship still in service when she was withdrawn in December 1963 after 45 years of service to the Line and sold for scrap in Hong Kong to Patt Manfield Co Ltd and arrived on February 4, 1964, for breaking up.

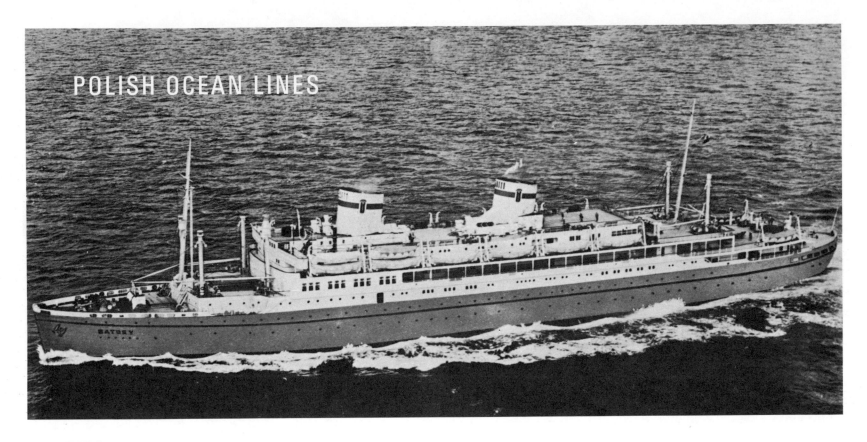

POLISH OCEAN LINES

BATORY

Builder: Cantieri Riuniti dell' Adriatico, Monfalcone, Italy.
Completed: April 1936.
Gross tonnage: 14287.
Dimensions: 526ft × 71ft. Depth 38ft.
Engines: Two nine-cylinder, two-stroke, single-acting Burmeister & Wain diesel.
Screws: Twin.
Watertight bulkheads: Nine.
Decks: Five.
Normal speed: 18 knots.
Passenger accommodation: 76 first and 740 tourist class. (Accommodations are combined into a single class of 800 when pleasure-cruising.)
Maiden voyage: Gdynia–Copenhagen–New York on May 18, 1936.
Last voyage for Polish Ocean Lines: London–Gdynia on May 29, 1969.

Employed in the Gdynia–Copenhagen–Southampton–Halifax–New York services and cruising. The Halifax call being eliminated eastbound. Requisitioned by the allies in 1939 as a transport and did not resume scheduled sailings until May 1947 from Gdynia to New York as a tourist-class ship. Commenced her last voyage from New York to Southampton, Copenhagen and Gdynia in January 1951 after having been denied docking facilities at the port of New York on the stipulation that she came from behind the Iron Curtain. Refitted for a new service from Gdynia to Southampton, via Suez Canal, Bombay and Karachi in August 1951. The *Batory* operated in this service until 1956 when she was overhauled at Bremerhaven, Germany, and placed in the Gdynia–Copenhagen–Southampton–Montreal service on August 26, 1957, and to Halifax in winter. A call at Le Havre was inaugurated in 1961. Withdrawn from service on June 1, 1969, and sold to the Gdansk District Board for use as a floating hotel at Gdynia, Poland. *(See Notes on p. 223.)*
Sister ship: *Pilsudski.*

PILSUDSKI

Builder: Cantieri Riuniti dell' Adriatico, Monfalcone, Italy.
Completed: August 1935.
Gross tonnage: 14294.
Dimensions: 526ft × 71ft. Depth 38ft.
Engines: Two nine-cylinder, two-stroke, single-acting oil.
Screws: Twin.
Watertight bulkheads: Nine.
Decks: Five.
Normal speed: 18 knots.
Passenger accommodation: 355 tourist and 404 third class.
Maiden voyage: Gdynia–New York in September 1935

Engaged in the Gdynia–Copenhagen–Southampton–New York service. She was refitted as an armed merchant cruiser in World War II and sunk by a German submarine off the Humber River, England, on November 26, 1939, with the loss of eight crew members.

Note: The *Pilsudski* and *Batory* were constructed for the Polish Ocean Lines by payments of Polish coal to the builders and the help of 12 countries who contributed to their construction.
Sister ship: *Batory.*

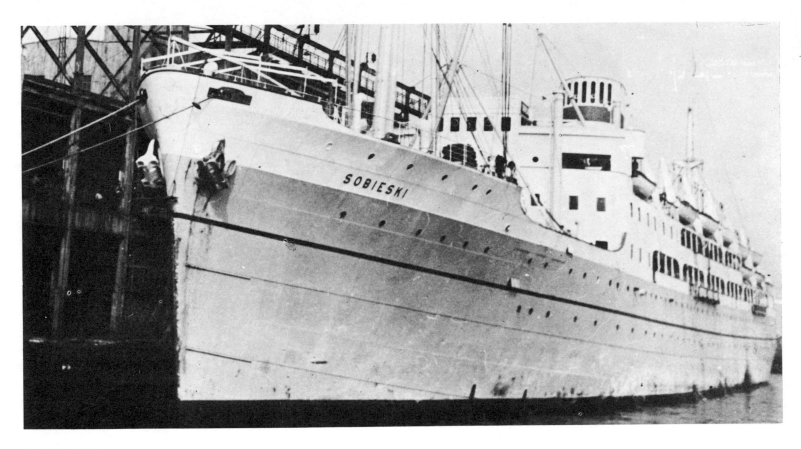

SOBIESKI

Builder: Swan, Hunter & Wigham Richardson Ltd, Newcastle-on-Tyne, England.
Completed: May 1939.
Gross tonnage: 11030.
Dimensions: 511ft × 67ft. Depth 67ft.
Engines: Two eight-cylinder, two-stroke, double-acting diesel.
Screws: Twin.
Watertight bulkheads: Eight.
Decks: Four.
Normal speed: 17 knots.
Passenger accommodation: 44 first and 860 tourist class.
Maiden voyage: Gdynia—Buenos Aires in June 1939.

She had been originally built for the South American trade. Commissioned by the allies during World War II as a transport and was fortunate in comparison with her sister *Chrobry* who also had been recently constructed when war broke out. Sold to Russia in March 1950 and renamed *Gruzia*. She is reportedly still in service.
Sister ship: *Chrobry*.

STEFAN BATORY

Builder: N.V. Wilton, Fijenoord, Schiedam, Netherlands.
Completed: July 1952.
Gross tonnage: 15024.
Dimensions: 503ft × 69ft. Depth 42ft.
Engines: Two steam turbines double-reduction geared.
Screws: Single.
Watertight bulkheads: Eight.
Decks: Four.
Normal speed: 16.50 knots.
Passenger accommodation: 39 first and 742 tourist class.
Maiden voyage: Gdynia–Copenhagen–Rotterdam–London–Montreal on April 11, 1969.
Officers and crew: 336.

Built for the Holland-America Line. Sold to the Polish Ocean Lines in December 1968 and renamed *Stefan Batory*. Employed in the Gdynia–Copenhagen–Rotterdam–London–Montreal service with a call at Southampton instead of London eastbound and cruising during the winter months to the West Indies from Montreal. Fully air-conditioned and equipped with motion stabilisers. She is the flagship of the Polish Ocean Lines and is presently in service.

PORTUGUESE LINE

IMPERIO

Builder: John Brown & Co Ltd, Clydebank, Glasgow, Scotland.
Completed: June 1948.
Gross tonnage: 13186.
Dimensions: 531ft × 68ft. Depth 44ft.
Engines: Four steam turbines, double-reduction geared.
Screws: Twin.

Collision bulkhead: One.
Watertight bulkheads: Eight.
Decks: Four.
Normal speed: 17 knots.
Officers and crew: 193.
Passenger accommodation: 114 first, 156 cabin and 118 tourist class.

Engaged in the Lisbon–Luanda–Beira trade with calls at other South African ports. She is equipped with every modern facility to ensure passenger comfort and has since the spring of 1970 been requisitioned by the Portuguese Government. *(See Notes on p. 223.)*
Sister ship: *Patria.*

INFANTE DOM HENRIQUE

Builder: Societe Anonyme, Cockerill-Ougree,
 Hoboken, Belgium.
Completed: September 1961.
Gross tonnage: 23306.
Dimensions: 642ft × 84ft. Depth 47ft.
Engines: Four steam turbines, double-reduction
 geared.
Screws: Twin.
Watertight bulkheads: Nine.
Decks: Five.
Normal speed: 20 knots.
Officers and crew: 328.
Passenger accommodation: 156 first and 862
 tourist class.

Engaged in the Lisbon—East African ports—Beira trade. She has a cargo capacity for 724553 cubic feet of grain, bales and refrigerated cargo. Equipped with motion stabilisers and fully air-conditioned. The *Infante Dom Henrique* is the Portugues Line's flagship. *(See Notes on p. 223.)*

PATRIA

Builders: John Brown & Co Ltd, Clydebank,
  Glasgow, Scotland.
Completed: December 1947.
Gross tonnage: 13196.
Dimensions: 531ft × 68ft. Depth 44ft.
Engines: Four steam turbines, double-
  reduction geared.
Screws: Twin.

Collision bulkhead: One.
Watertight bulkheads: Eight.
Decks: Four.
Normal speed: 17 knots.
Officers and crew: 193.
Passenger accommodation: 114 first, 160
  cabin and 118 tourist class.
Last voyage: March 7, 1973.

Engaged in the Lisbon—Luanda—Beira trade. She
is equipped with every modern facility to ensure
passenger comfort. *(See Notes on p. 223.)*
Sister ship: *Imperio.*

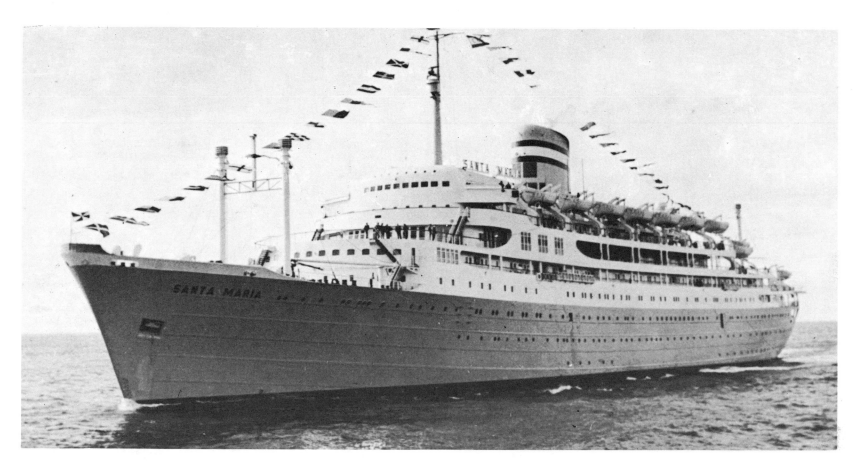

SANTA MARIA

Builder: Societe Anonyme, John Cockerill, Hoboken, Belgium.
Completed: September 1953.
Gross tonnage: 20906.
Dimensions: 609ft × 76ft. Depth 43ft.
Engines: Six steam turbines, double-reduction geared.
Screws: Twin.
Watertight bulkheads: Nine.
Decks: Five.
Normal speed: 20 knots.
Officers and crew: 369.
Passenger accommodation: 156 first, 226 cabin and 696 tourist class.
Maiden voyage to the U.S.: Arrived at Port Everglades on January 14, 1957.
Last voyage: From Lisbon on March 15, 1973.

Employed in the Lisbon–Vigo–Madeira–Tenerife–La Guaira–Curaçao–Fort Lauderdale service in the winter season with the elimination of the calls at La Guaira and Curacao during the summer months. On the morning of January 22, 1961, the *Santa Maria* was seized by 24 Spanish and Portuguese rebels at 01.30am. In the struggle to take the

ship one crew member was killed and two others wounded. The ship hove to off the Brazilian coast while being hunted by air and sea until spotted and forced to land at Recife, Brazil, on February 2. She is equipped with motion stabilisers and is fully air-conditioned. *(See Notes on p. 223.)*
Sister ship: *Vera Cruz.*

UIGE

Builder: Societe Anonyme, John Cockerill,
Hoboken, Belgium.
Completed: July 1954.
Gross tonnage: 10001.
Dimensions: 477ft × 63ft. Depth 37ft.
Engines: One eight-cylinder, two-stroke, single-
acting B & W oil.
Screws: Single.
Watertight bulkheads: Seven.
Decks: Four.
Normal speed: 16 knots.
Officers and crew: 159.
Passenger accommodation: 78 first and 493
tourist class.

Engaged in the Lisbon–Angola–Mozambique
trade. She is equipped with every modern facility
to ensure passenger comfort and is presently in
the Portugal–Africa trade.

VERA CRUZ

Builder: Societe Anonyme, John Cockerill, Hoboken, Belgium.
Completed: February 1952.
Gross tonnage: 21765.
Dimensions: 610ft × 76ft. Depth 43ft.
Engines: Six steam turbines double-reduction geared.
Screws: Twin.
Watertight bulkheads: Nine.
Decks: Five.
Normal speed: 20 knots.
Officers and crew: 356.
Passenger accommodation: 148 first, 250 cabin, and 760 tourist class.
Last voyage: From Lisbon on January 7, 1973.

Employed in the Lisbon—Canary Islands—Rio de Janeiro and several other ports along the South American and East African continents. She is equipped with motion stabilisers and is fully air-conditioned. *(See Notes on p. 223.)*
Note: The *Vera Cruz* and the *Santa Maria* also call at Port Everglades monthly.
Sister ship: *Santa Maria.*

SPANISH LINE

ARGENTINA

Builder: Swan, Hunter & Wigham Richardson Ltd, Wallsend-on-Tyne, England.
Completed: February 1913.
Gross tonnage: 10137.
Dimensions: 480ft. × 61ft. Depth 36ft.
Engines: Two four-cylinder, quadruple-expansion engines and two low-pressure turbines.
Screws: Quadruple.
Watertight bulkheads: Nine.
Decks: Four.
Normal speed: 17 knots.
Passenger accommodation: 250 first, 100 second and 75 third class.

She was christened *Reina Victoria Eugenia*. Renamed *Argentina* in 1931. Engaged in the Spain–Havana–Vera Cruz service and Spain–New York run. Reallocated to the Spain–South American trade in 1931. Sunk by an air attack at Barcelona, Spain, between January 16 and 23, 1939, during the Spanish Civil War. Refloated and sold for scrap in 1945.
Sister ship: *Uruguay.*

BEGONA

Builder: Bethlehem-Fairfield Yard, Baltimore, Maryland, USA.
Completed: 1945.
Gross tonnage: 10139.
Dimensions: 455ft × 62ft. Depth 38ft.
Engines: Two steam turbines, double-reduction geared.
Screws: Single.
Watertight bulkhead: Seven.
Decks: Three.
Normal speed: 17.50 knots.
Officers and crew: 200.
Passenger accommodation: 123 special tourist and 830 tourist class.
Last voyage for Spanish Line: Southampton—Vigo—Tenerife—Port of Spain—Trinidad—La Guaira—Kingston on September 27, 1974.

Built for the United States Department of Commerce and christened *Vassar Victory*. Sold to the Sitmar Line in 1947 and renamed *Castelbianco; Castel Bianco* in 1953. Sold to the Spanish Line in 1957 and renamed *Begona*. Employed in the Genoa—Naples—Coruna—Vigo—Canary Islands—Central America—Cuba route until May 1958 when she was reallocated to the Southampton—Santander—Coruna—Vigo—Tenerife—Trinidad—La Guaira—Curacao—Kingston service calling at San Juan instead of Curacao homeward. She is equipped with motion stabilisers and is fully air-conditioned. The *Begona* is the Spanish Line's flagship. *(See Notes on p. 223.)*
Sister ship: *Montserrat*.

II COVADONGA

Builder: Compania Euskalduna, Bilbao, Spain.
Completed: August 1953.
Gross tonnage: 10226.
Dimensions: 487ft × 62ft. Depth 40ft.
Engines: One ten-cylinder, two-stroke, single-acting Sulzer diesel engine.
Screws: Single.
Watertight bulkheads: Eight.
Decks: Three.
Normal speed: 16.50 knots.
Officers and crew: 135.
Passenger accommodation: 105 first and 248 tourist class.
Maiden voyage: Bilbao–Santander–Gijon–Vigo Lisbon–New York–Havana–Vera Cruz on August 27, 1953.
Last voyage for Spanish Line: Bilbao–Vigo–Lisbon–San Juan–Vera Cruz–Tampico–Miami–Bilbao on December 3, 1972.

She was launched as the *Monasterio de la Rabida*. She was originally laid down as a cargo liner for the Empresa Nacional Elcano, but purchased by the Spanish Line before completion. Renamed *Covadonga* in the same year before entering service. Engaged in the Bilbao–Santander–Gijon–Vigo–Lisbon–San Juan–Vera Cruz–Norfolk, Va.– New York route westbound and New York–La Coruna–Gijon–Santander–Bilbao homeward. She formerly made a call at Cadiz and Havana, but eliminated these ports in 1962.
(See Notes on p. 223.)
Sister ship: *Guadalupe*.

II CRISTOBAL COLON

Builder: Sociedad Espanola de Construccion
   Naval, Ferrol, Spain.
Completed: September 1923.
Gross tonnage: 10833.
Dimensions: 499ft × 61ft. Depth 36ft.
Engines: Four steam turbines, single-reduction
geared.
Screws: Twin.
Watertight bulkheads: Ten.
Decks: Three.
Normal speed: 17 knots.
Passenger accommodation: 1100 in first,
   second and third class.

Engaged in the Spain–New York–Havana trade. At the outbreak of the Spanish Civil War in July 1936 the *Cristobal Colon* was ordered to return to Spain by the government while on an eastbound voyage. The ship was taken over by some insurrectionists among the crew and she was diverted to Southampton to disembark her passengers. After calling at Cardiff, Wales, she sailed for Vera Cruz and was wrecked on North Rock, Bermuda, on October 24, 1936, by the crew.
Sister ship: *Habana.*

GUADALUPE

Builder: Sociedad Espanola de Construccion Naval, Bilbao, Spain.
Completed: March 1953.
Gross tonnage: 10226.
Dimensions: 487ft × 62ft. Depth 40ft.
Engines: One ten-cylinder, two-stroke, single-acting Sulzer diesel.
Screws: Single.
Watertight bulkheads: Eight.
Decks: Three.
Normal speed: 16.50 knots.
Officers and crew: 135.
Passenger accommodation: 105 first and 244 tourist class.
Maiden voyage: Bilbao–Santander–Gijon–Vigo–Lisbon–New York–Havana–Vera Cruz on March 21, 1953.
Last voyage: Bilbao–Vigo–Lisbon–San Juan–Vera Cruz–Miami–Port Arthur–Aviles–Bilbao on January 5, 1973.

She was launched as the *Monasterio de Guadalupe*. Originally laid down as a cargo liner for the Empress Nacional Elcano, but purchased by the Spanish Line before completion. Her name was then contracted to *Guadalupe* before entering service. Employed in the Bilbao–Santander–Gijon–Vigo–Lisbon–San Juan–Vera Cruz–Norfolk, Va.–New York route outward and New York–La Coruna–Gijon–Santander–Bilbao homeward. She formerly made a call at Cadiz and Havana, but eliminated these ports in 1962.
(See Notes on p. 223.)
Sister ship: *Covadonga*.

II HABANA

Builder: Sociedad Espanola de Construccion
Naval, Bilbao, Spain.
Completed: August 1923.
Gross tonnage: 10551.
Dimensions: 500ft × 61ft. Depth 36ft.
Engines: Four steam turbines, single-reduction
geared.
Screws: Twin.
Watertight bulkheads: Ten.
Decks: Three.
Normal speed: 16 knots.
Passenger accommodation: 101 in a single
first-class capacity.

She was christened *Alfonso XIII*. Renamed
Habana in 1931. Engaged in the Spain–New York–
Havana trade. Laid up at Bordeaux, France, during
the Spanish Civil War. She was gutted by fire at
Bilbao, Spain, in 1943 and reconstructed as a
cargo ship with a limited accommodation for 12
persons. Overhauled at the Todd Brooklyn Ship-
yard, New York, and given the present passenger

complement in 1947. At the time of her construction she had carried 1100 in three classes. Re-
entered service in April 1947 and sold to the
Pescanova SA on May 12, 1962, and renamed
Galicia after another refitting, this time as a fish
factory ship. Recently in operation. The above
photo is the *Habana* as a cargo vessel.
Sister ship: *Cristobal Colon.*

URUGUAY

Builder: William Denny & Bros Ltd, Dumbarton, Scotland.
Completed: March 1913.
Gross tonnage: 10348.
Dimensions: 482ft × 61ft. Depth 36ft.
Engines: Two three-cylinder, triple expansion.
Screws: Triple.
Watertight bulkheads: Eight.
Decks: Four.
Normal speed: 17 knots. (Attained a speed of 18.64 knots on her trial runs.)
Passenger accommodation: 250 first, 100 second and 75 third class.

She was christened *Infanta Isable de Borbon*. Renamed *Uruguay* in 1931. Engaged in the Spain–Havana–Vera Cruz service and Spain–New York run. Reallocated to the Spain–South American trade in 1931 and sunk by an air attack at Valencia, Spain, between January 16 and 23, 1939, during the Spanish Civil War. Refloated on July 27, 1942, and sold for scrap.
Sister ship: *Argentina*.

Nightfall finds the Swedish-American Liners *Gripsholm* and *Kungsholm* at pier ninety-seven.

SWEDISH-AMERICAN LINE

DROTTNINGHOLM

Builder: Alexander Stephen & Sons, Ltd, Glasgow, Scotland.
Completed: April 1905.
Gross tonnage: 11055.
Dimensions: 538ft × 60ft. Depth 41ft.
Engines: Steam turbines, single-reduction geared.
Screws: Triple.
Watertight bulkheads: Seven.
Decks: Four.
Normal speed: 17.50 knots.
Officers and crew: 219.
Passenger accommodation: 426 first, 286 second and 800 third class.
Maiden voyage: Gothenburg—New York, arriving on June 9, 1920.

Built for the Allan Line and christened *Virginian*. Sold to the Canadian Pacific Line in 1916. Resold to the Swedish-American Line in early 1920 and renamed *Drottningholm*. Engaged in the Gothenburg—Copenhagen—New York service. Converted to oil-firing and her original Parson turbines replaced by the presently stated type of propulsion in 1922. In April 1942 she was chartered by the allies to bring diplomats across the Atlantic and was later used for repatriation work under the office of the International Red Cross. Resumed scheduled sailings in March 1946 from Gothenburg to New York and was the first liner to commence peacetime voyages since the war. She was the first Atlantic turbine-driven liner when built for the Allan Line. Made her 440th and last voyage for the Swedish-American Line in February 1948 and was sold to the Home Lines in the same month and renamed *Brasil: Homeland* in 1951. Sold for scrap at Trieste, Italy, in 1955 after a long service of 50 years under three flags, Reprieved when she was resold to the South Atlantic Lines the following year and retained until 1962.

I GRIPSHOLM

Builder: W. G. Armstrong, Whitworth & Co Ltd, Newcastle-on-Tyne, England.
Completed: November 1925.
Gross tonnage: 19105.
Dimensions: 590ft × 74ft. Depth 43ft.
Engines: Two six-cylinder, four-stroke, double-acting Burmeister & Wain diesel.
Screws: Twin.
Watertight bulkheads: Ten.
Decks: Five.
Normal speed: 16 knots.
Officers and crew: 350.
Passenger accommodation: 210 first and 710 tourist class.
Maiden voyage: Gothenburg–New York on November 21, 1925.

Engaged in the Gothenburg–Copenhagen–New York service and cruising. In February 1927 she made her first extensive cruise to the Mediterranean and made an annual cruise to South America. In March 1942 she was chartered by the United States Government until March 1946 at a cost of $17000 a day. After the war she carried Japanese, Germans, and Italians, to their fatherland and repatriated allies on her return trips while under the office of the International Red Cross. During this extensive duty of repatriation she carried over 27000 people and covered over 120000 miles which made her the most well-known mercy ship of the war. Re-entered service in March 1946 from New York to Gothenburg. On July 18, 1952,

she rescued 45 persons from the burning Norwegian freighter *Black Hawk* 75 miles off New York. The *Gripsholm* was the first transatlantic liner to be driven by diesel engines. Refitted in 1949 at Kiel, Germany, and given a new stem with an increase in length from 574ft to 590ft and larger funnels. Commenced her last voyage for the Swedish-American Line on December 29, 1953, from Gothenburg to New York and was sold to the North German Lloyd in January 1954 with the Swedish-American Line retaining half ownership. Subsequently sold in full to the North German Lloyd in January 1955 and renamed *Berlin*. Sold for scrap in Italy in October 1966.

II GRIPSHOLM

Builder: Ansaldo SpA Cantieri Navale, Sestri, Genoa, Italy.
Completed: April 1957.
Gross tonnage: 23216.
Dimensions: 631ft × 82ft. Depth 50ft.
Engines: Two nine-cylinder, two-stroke, single-acting diesel.
Screws: Twin.
Watertight bulkheads: Eleven.
Decks: Five.
Normal speed: 18 knots.
Officers and crew: 350.
Passenger accommodation: 175 first and 682 tourist class. (Accommodations are restricted to 450 when pleasure-cruising.)
Maiden voyage: Gothenburg–Copenhagen–Halifax–New York on May 14, 1957.
Last voyage: New York–Copenhagen–Gothenburg on August 26, 1975.

Engaged in the Gothenburg–Copenhagen–New York run and cruising. In 1966 she was transferred to cruise services with the advent of the new *Kungsholm*. Presently in cruise services to all five continents throughout the year with a few transatlantic voyages when the *Kungsholm* is drydocked once every year. The *Gripsholm*'s forefunnel is a dummy, but conceals a staircase leading to a passenger observation platform at the top. She is fully air-conditioned and is equipped with motion stabilisers. Her cargo capacity is 82500 cubic feet and has a water evaporator capable of 175 tons per day. Built with a stylish clipper bow she is popularly known as the 'Golden Yacht'. *(See Notes on p. 223.)*

II KUNGSHOLM

Builder: Blohm & Voss, Hamburg, Germany.
Completed: November 1928.
Gross tonnage: 20067.
Dimensions: 609ft × 78ft. Depth 43ft.
Engines: Two eight-cylinder, four-stroke, double-acting Burmeister & Wain diesel.
Screws: Twin.
Watertight bulkheads: Ten.
Decks: Five.
Normal speed: 17.50 knots.
Officers and crew: 344.
Passenger accommodation: 115 first, 489 second and 940 third class.
Maiden voyage: Gothenburg–New York on November 24, 1928.

Employed in the Gothenburg–Copenhagen–New York service and pleasure-cruising. In 1940 she was sent cruising from the port of New York to the West Indies until seized by the United States on January 13, 1941, and converted into a transport. She was officially sold to the US Government on January 2, 1942, and sailed under the name of *John Ericsson* from the time of her seizure. During her services as an American transport she carried over 170000 troops across the Atlantic and after the war was used as a warbride ship with new and different accommodations for 279 mothers and 177 babies. She also made a few voyages under the management of the United States Lines during the peacetime period. Caught fire at New York in March 1947 and was sold back to the Swedish-American Line in July. Sailed for the Ansaldo shipyards in Genoa, Italy, in December 1947 to be repaired. Sold to the Home Lines in the same year at cost of repairs consideration and renamed *Italia*. Resold to an American firm in 1964 and converted to a 500-room hotel at Freeport, Bahamas, and renamed the 'Imperial Bahama Hotel'. Offered up for sale in June 1965 and when no buyers turned up was sold for scrap to Spanish shipbreakers in 1966.

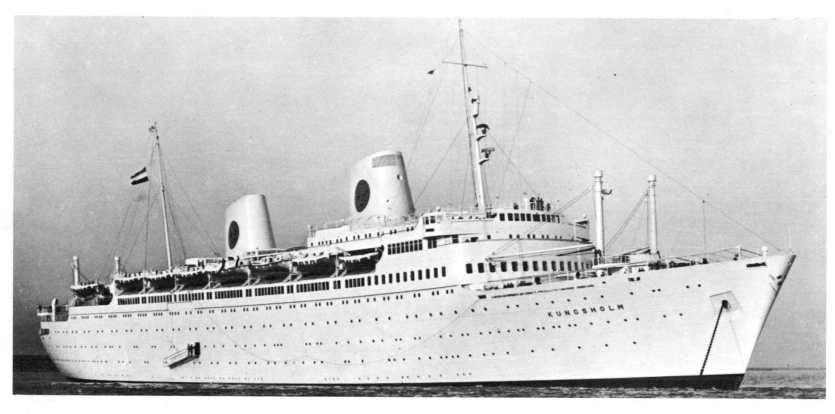

III KUNGSHOLM

Builder: De Schelde N.V.,Flushing, Netherlands.
Completed: October 1953.
Gross tonnage: 21164.
Dimensions: 60ft ×77ft. Depth 49ft.
Engines: Two eight-cylinder, two-stroke
single-acting Burmeister & Wain diesel.
Screws: Twin.
Collision bulkhead: One.
Watertight bulkheads: Eight.
Decks: Five.
Normal speed: 19 knots.
Officers and crew: 355.
Passenger accommodation: 176 first and 626
tourist class. (Accommodations are reduced to
400 when in cruise services.)
Maiden voyage: Gothenburg—Copenhagen—
New York on November 24, 1953.

Engaged in the Gothenburg—Copenhagen—New York run with cruises all over the world. In January 1955 she made her first round-the-world cruise in the history of the Swedish-American Line in 97 days and calling at 21 ports. Fitted with motion stabilisers in 1961. She is fully air-conditioned and her masts are telescopic so they may be retracted to permit passage under any low bridges. All cabins are outside and furnished with bath or shower and telephone. Sold to the North German Lloyd in October 1965 with the building of the new *Kungsholm* almost completed and renamed *Europa*. Presently in their service.

IV KUNGSHOLM

Builder: John Brown & Co Ltd, Clydebank,
Glasgow, Scotland.
Completed: March 1966.
Gross tonnage: 26678.
Dimensions: 660ft × 87ft. Depth 51ft.
Engines: Two nine-cylinder, two-stroke, single-
acting diesel.
Screws: Twin.
Collision bulkhead: One.
Watertight bulkheads: Nine.
Decks: Five.
Normal speed: 21 knots
Officers and crew: 450.
Passenger accommodation: 108 first and 642
tourist class. (Accommodations are limited to
450 when in cruise services.)
Maiden voyage: Gothenburg–Copenhagen–
New York on April 22, 1966.
Last voyage: New York–Hamilton, Bermuda–Prince
Edward Island–Quebec–Halifax on August 28,
1975.

Engaged in the Gothenburg–Copenhagen–New York service with cruises all over the world during most of the year. The *Kungsholm's* forward funnel is a dummy and is used as a store room. On January 15, 1971, she made a 94-day cruise to the Pacific and called at 23 ports. She is the Swedish-American Line's flagship. Equipped with motion stabilisers and fully air-conditioned.
(See Notes on p. 223.)

I STOCKHOLM

Builder: Blohm & Voss, Hamburg, Germany.
Completed: May 1900.
Gross tonnage: 12835.
Dimensions: 571ft × 62ft. Depth 38ft.
Engines: Two three-cylinder, triple expansion.
Screws: Twin.
Watertight bulkheads: Ten.
Decks: Four.
Normal speed: 15 knots.
Officers and crew: 200.
Passenger accommodation: 210 first, 210
  second and 700 third class.
Maiden voyage: Gothenburg–New York on
  December 11, 1915.

Built for the Holland-America Line and christened
Potsdam. Sold to the Swedish-American Line in
September 1915 and renamed *Stockholm*. The
Stockholm had a promenade deck 195ft long.
Employed in the Gothenburg–Copenhagen–New
York run and was managed by the A. Carlander &
V. R. Olburs Shipping Co from 1926 until 1928
when she was sold to the Norwegian firm Odd Co,

AS and converted to a whale factory ship and renamed *Solgimt*. Captured by the German raider
Pinguin in the Antarctic and taken to occupied
France during World War II where she was used as
a tanker. Scuttled by the Germans at Cherbourg,
France, in June 1944. When it became impossible
to refloat her she was blown up on August 30,
1946.

IV STOCKHOLM

Builder: A.B. Gotaverken, Gothenburg, Sweden.
Completed: February 1948.
Gross tonnage: 12396.
Dimensions: 525ft × 69ft. Depth 39ft.
Engines: Two eight-cylinder, two-stroke, single-acting Gotaverken diesel.
Screws: Twin.
Decks: Three.
Normal speed: 19 knots.
Officers and crew: 219.
Passenger accommodation: 28 first and 557 tourist; 350 in one class when cruising.
Maiden voyage: Gothenburg–New York on February 21, 1948.
Last voyage for Swedish-American Line: New York–Halifax–Bremerhaven–Copenhagen–Gothenburg on December 4, 1959.

Classified as a cargo-passenger liner and engaged in the Gothenburg–Copenhagen–New York service. Refitted in November 1953 for the present enlarged passenger complement and fitted with Denny-Brown gyro stabilisers in 1956. On the night of July 25, 1956, the *Stockholm* rammed the Italian liner *Andrea Doria* in a calm fog at 11.22pm off the Nantucket Shoals. The reinforced ice-breaker bow of the *Stockholm* pierced her starboard side and sank the lovely ship in the matter of an hour. The *Stockholm* incurred a loss of five lives of her crew who were in their quarters forward when the collision occurred. The *Stockholm*'s lifeboats were sent to pick up survivors from the *Doria* and proceeded to New York where she was laid up for repairs. A formal inquiry found both ships at fault in relation to the navigation laws concerning altering the course of a ship when approaching another ship on the radar screen which both ships failed to do on the night of July 25, 1956. Resumed services from New York to Copenhagen and Gothenburg on December 8, 1956. Sold to the Freier Deutsche Gerwerkschafts-Bund on January 1, 1960, and renamed *Volkerfreundschaft*. Presently in their service.
Note: The *Stockholm* was the first passenger liner ever built in Sweden for the Line.

UNITED STATES LINES

I AMERICA

Builder: Harland & Wolff Ltd, Belfast, Ireland.
Completed: April 1905.
Gross tonnage: 21329.
Dimensions: 687ft×74ft. Depth 52ft.
Engines: Two four-cylinder, quadruple expansion.
Screws: Twin.
Watertight bulkheads: Twelve.
Decks: Five.
Normal speed: 17.75 knots.
Passenger accommodation: 693 cabin and 1240 tourist and third class.
Maiden voyage: New York—Bremen—Danzig on August 27, 1921.

Built for the Hamburg-America Line and christened *Amerika*. Seized by the United States at Boston, Massachusetts, in April 1917. Converted to a transport with her name anglicised to *America* in October 1918. On the night before entering service as a troopship the *America* sank at her pier at New York when some valves had been left open accidentally. She was refloated and used for repatriation work rather than trooping. Transferred to the US Mail Line in July 1921 and subsequently to the United States Lines on August 31, 1921. Engaged in the New York–Channel ports–Bremen service year-round. Rebuilt in 1926 after being almost completely destroyed by fire at Newport News, Virginia. Returned to her owners, the US Department of Commerce, in 1931 and laid up in the James River, Virginia, until recommissioned for troop work in 1941 under the name of *Edmund B. Alexander*. Refitted for oil fuel in 1942 and her two funnels replaced by a single squat one. Laid up in the Hudson River after the war as a reserve ship. Sold for scrap at Baltimore, Maryland, in 1956 to the Bethlehem Steel Corporation and broken up by 1957.

Note: The *America* was the first ship to have an *à la carte* restaurant and ranked very high in her day as a luxury liner.

II AMERICA

Builder: Newport News Shipbuilding & Drydock Co, Newport News, Virginia, United States.
Completed: July 1940.
Gross tonnage: 33961.
Dimensions: 723ft × 94ft. Depth 56ft.
Engines: Six steam turbines, high-pressure, double-reduction geared; intermediate-pressure and low-pressure, single-reduction geared.
Screws: Twin.
Watertight bulkheads: Fourteen.
Decks: Five.
Normal speed: 22.50 knots.
Passenger accommodation: 516 first and 530 tourist class.
Maiden voyage: New York—St. Thomas—San Juan—Port au Prince—Havana on August 10, 1940.
Officers and crew: 675.

Engaged in the New York—Cobh—Le Havre—Southampton—Bremerhaven service, and cruising. The *America* was requisitioned for troop work in 1941 and ran under the name of *West Point*. Resumed transatlantic sailings on November 14, 1946, from New York to Cobh, Southampton and Le Havre under her original name. On her first voyage out she made the run from Ambrose Lighthouse to Daunt's Lightship in 4 days, 22 hours and 22 minutes at a speed of 24.54 knots. During the course of the war she had carried over 400000 troops of allies and steamed over 500000 miles. She inaugurated the call at Bremerhaven since October 1951. Sold to the Chandris Lines in November 1964 and renamed *Australis*.
(See Notes on p. 223.)

GEORGE WASHINGTON

Builder: A.G. Vulkan, Stettin, Germany.
Completed: June 1909.
Gross tonnage: 23788.
Dimensions: 722ft × 78ft. Depth 50ft.
Engines: Two four-cylinder, quadruple expansion.
Screws: Twin.
Watertight bulkheads: Twelve.
Decks: Six.
Normal speed: 18.50 knots.
Passenger accommodation: 500 first, 377 cabin, 614 third and 1432 steerage.
Maiden voyage: New York—Bremen on September 3, 1921.

Built for the North German Lloyd. Interned at New York in 1914 and seized by the United States Government in April 1917 and converted to a troopship. Returned to the United States Shipping Board in 1919 and managed for them by the United States Mail Line from August 1920 until the collapse of the Line on August 31, 1921, when she was handed over to the newly born United States Lines. Engaged in the New York—Channel ports—Bremen service year-round. She was returned to the United States Shipping Board in September 1932 and laid up in the Patuxent River, Maryland, as a reserve troopship. Taken over by the British in 1940 and brought to Halifax, Nova Scotia, for refitting as a transport and renamed *Catlin* in 1941. Britain decided not to use her and she was returned to the United States in April 1942 and recovered her original name. Completed by the United States for war purposes with conversion to oil-firing; the elimination of a funnel and new accommodation for 6500 armed men. Entered service as a troopship in April 1943 and was decommissioned in May 1947 and offered up for sale. When no buyers appeared she was laid up at Baltimore where she was destroyed by fire off Hawkins Point on January 16, 1951. The remaining hulk was sold for scrap to the Boston Metal Co at Baltimore, Maryland, where breaking up commenced on February 14, 1951. During her career as a liner and her war services the *George Washington* carried more than 160000 persons and steamed over 185000 miles.

LEVIATHAN

Builder: Blohm & Voss, Hamburg, Germany.
Completed: May 1914.
Gross tonnage: 48943.
Dimensions: 950ft × 100ft. Depth 64ft.
Engines: Four sets of steam turbines.
Screws: Quadruple.
Watertight bulkheads: Thirteen.
Decks: Seven.
Normal speed: 24 knots. (Attained a speed of 27.07 knots on her trial runs.)
Officers and crew: 1150.
Passenger accommodation: 978 first, 548 second and 2117 third class.
Maiden voyage: New York–Cherbourg– Southampton on July 4, 1923.

Built for the Hamburg-America Line and christened *Vaterland*. Interned at New York after her second voyage for Hapag. Seized by the United States on April 4, 1917 and renamed *Leviathan* after she was commissioned as a transport. Transferred to the United States Lines by the US Shipping Board in 1923. *Leviathan* was converted to oil-firing in September 1919 and was once again reconditioned in 1923 when her gross tonnage was increased to 59957 making her the largest ship in the world. Tonnage was soon reduced to the present figure in 1931 when it had cost the owners over $2 million in dry dock and harbour dues due to her size. Engaged in the New York–Channel ports–Bremen service. In her career as a US Transport she carried as many as ten thousand troops on each trip and was known by the American troops as the 'Levi Nathan'. Prohibition and the depression caused the *Leviathan* to be withdrawn from service in December 1933. In June 1934 she made five round trips and her last on September 8, 1934, from Southampton to Le Havre and New York. Sold for scrap in January 1938 and left New York for the last time on January 25 steaming for the shipbreaker's yard at Rosyth, Scotland. As majestic as the *Leviathan* was to look upon she never won acclaim with the American people.

MANHATTAN

Builder: New York Shipbuilding Corporation,
Camden, New Jersey.
Completed: 1932.
Gross tonnage: 24289.
Dimensions: 705ft×86ft. Depth 47ft.
Engines: Six steam turbines, single-reduction
geared.
Screws: Twin.
Watertight bulkheads: Eleven.
Decks: Six.
Normal speed: 20 knots.
Passenger accommodation: 500 cabin, 500
tourist and 200 third class.
Maiden voyage: New York–Cobh–Plymouth–
Le Havre–Hamburg on August 10, 1932.

Engaged in the New York–Channel ports–Hamburg route and ran to Genoa from January 1940 until July of that year because of the impending crisis over Northern Europe at the time. In January 1941 the *Manhattan* ran aground off the east coast of Florida while on a cruise and remained fixed for 22 days, her 199 passengers having been removed by the Coast Guard cutter *Vigilante* which took them to Palm Beach where they could make other arrangements for their respective destinations. The *Manhattan* was towed to New York for repairs which, when completed, amounted to almost $2 million dollars. Requisitioned for troop service in 1941 and renamed *Wakefield*. Caught fire on September 3, 1942, while in a westbound convoy and was abandoned, but later taken to Boston and rebuilt. Resumed troop service in April 1944. With the conclusion of World War II the *Manhattan*, along with her sister the *Washington*, were destined never to sail again as luxury liners for the United States Lines and the *Manhattan* was laid up in the Hudson as a reserve ship by the US Department of Commerce, where she slowly rusted away until sold for scrap at Kearny, New Jersey, in July 1964.

Sister ship: *Washington*.

PRESIDENT ADAMS

Builder: New York Shipbuilding Corporation, Camden, New Jersey.
Completed: April 1921.
Gross tonnage: 10558.
Dimensions: 522ft × 62ft. Depth 42ft.
Engines: Two four-cylinder, triple expansion.
Screws: Twin.
Watertight bulkheads: Thirteen.
Decks: Three.
Normal speed: 14 knots.
Passenger accommodation: 140 in a single class.
Maiden voyage: New York—Boulogne—London on September 6, 1921, as *President Adams*.

Built for the United States Government and christened *Centennial State*. Managed by the US Mail Line until taken over by the United States Lines in August 31, 1921. Renamed *President Adams* in 1922. Engaged in the New York—London service until sold to the Dollar Line in September 1923 and transferred to them in early 1924. Passed to the American President Lines in 1938 and re- named *President Grant* in 1939. Struck a sub- merged reef in the South Pacific while transporting troops. The ship was fixed on the reef and her crew laboured for almost a hundred days to free her. When nearly completed, a great wave struck and split her in two on February 26, 1944.
Sister ships: *President Garfield, President Mon- roe, President Polk,* and *President Van Buren.*

PRESIDENT ARTHUR

Builder: A.G. Vulkan, Stettin, Germany.
Completed: September 1900.
Gross tonnage: 10421.
Dimensions: 523ft × 60ft. Depth 38ft.
Engines: Two four-cylinder, quadruple
   expansion.
Screws: Twin.
Watertight bulkheads: Thirteen.
Decks: Four.
Normal speed: 15 knots.
Passenger accommodation: First, second and
   third class.
Maiden voyage: New York—Bremen—Danzig on
   September 15, 1921.

Built for the Hamburg-America Line and christened *Kiautschou*. Sold to the North German Lloyd in 1903 and renamed *Prinzess Alice*. Seized by the United States Government at Manila, Philippines, in 1917 and renamed *Princess Matoika* for transport work. Transferred to the United States Mail Line in 1921 for management and subsequently to the United States Lines after five voyages when the US Mail Line collapsed on August 31, of that year. Renamed *President Arthur* in 1922. Engaged in the New York—Plymouth—Cherbourg—Bremen run eastbound and called at Southampton—Cherbourg—Cobh westbound. Withdrawn from service in the autumn of 1924 and chartered to the American-Palestine Line in 1925 who inaugurated service to Naples and Haifa on March 13. Sold to the Palace Line in 1926 and renamed *White Palace*. In 1927 she was resold once again to the Los Angeles Steamship Co and renamed *City of Honolulu*. Damaged by fire on May 25, 1930, at Honolulu she was able to make the trip back to Los Angeles and was laid up to rest after having sailed under many houseflags and was sold for scrap in way-off Japan in 1933.

PRESIDENT GARFIELD

Builder: New York Shipbuilding Corporation, Camden, New Jersey.
Completed: June 1921.
Gross tonnage: 10558.
Dimensions: 522ft × 62ft. Depth 42ft.
Engines: Two four-cylinder, triple expansion.
Screws: Twin.
Watertight bulkheads: Thirteen.
Decks: Three.
Normal speed: 14 knots.
Passenger accommodation: 140 in a single class.
Maiden voyage: New York—Queenstown—Plymouth—Cherbourg—London on May 31, 1922, as *President Garfield.*

Built for the United States Government and christened *Blue Hen State.* Managed by the US Mail Line until taken over by the United States Lines in August 31, 1921. Renamed *President Garfield* in 1922. Employed in the New York—London service. Sold to the Dollar Line in September 1923 and delivered in early 1924. Consolidated into the American President Lines in 1938 and renamed *President Madison* the following year. Requisitioned as a transport in World War II and renamed *Kenmore,* shortly afterwards she was reconverted to a hospital ship in 1942 under the name of *Refuge.* Sold for scrap in 1948.
Sister ships: *President Adams, President Monroe, President Polk,* and *President Van Buren.*

PRESIDENT HARDING

Builder: New York Shipbuilding Corporation, Camden, New Jersey, USA.
Completed: December 1921.
Gross tonnage: 13869.
Dimensions: 535ft × 72ft. Depth 41ft.
Engines: Four steam turbines, single-reduction geared.
Screws: Twin.
Normal speed: 18 knots.
Passenger accommodation: 320 cabin and 324 third class.
Maiden voyage: New York—Plymouth—Cherbourg—Bremen on March 25, 1922, as *Lone Star State*.

Built for the United States Government and christened *Lone Star State*. Transferred to the United States Lines in 1922 and renamed *President Taft* in May 1922; *President Harding* in late 1922. Engaged in the New York—Cobh—London service until mid-1932 when she was reallocated to the New York—Plymouth—Le Havre—Hamburg run eastbound and calling at Le Havre—Southampton—Cobh westbound. She is classified as a cargo-passenger liner. Sold to the Antwerp Navigation Co in February 1940 and renamed *Ville de Burges*. Following this transfer, which was enacted with the Belgian company so that American vessels might trade in the war zone area, she ceased to carry passengers. Sunk by Nazi bombers in the River Scheldt, Holland, on May 14, 1940.
Sister ship: *President Roosevelt.*

PRESIDENT MONROE

Builder: New York Shipbuilding Corporation, Camden, New Jersey.
Completed: August 1920.
Gross tonnage: 10533.
Dimensions: 522ft × 62ft. Depth 42ft.
Engines: Two four-cylinder, triple expansion.
Screws: Twin.
Watertight bulkheads: Thirteen.
Decks: Three.
Normal speed: 14 knots.
Passenger accommodation: 140 in a single class.
Maiden voyage: New York—Boulogne—London on October 25, 1921.

Built for the United States Government and christened *Panhandle State*. Managed by the US Mail Line until taken over by the United States Lines in August 31, 1921. Renamed *President Monroe* in 1922. Employed in the New York—London service until sold to the Dollar Line in September 1923 and delivered to them in early 1924. Passed on to the American President Lines in 1938 when the Dollar Line was merged with the new company and renamed *President Buchanan* in 1940. Converted to a hospital ship during World War II and renamed *Emily H. Weder*. Sold for scrap in 1948.
Sister ships: *President Adams, President Garfield, President Polk,* and *President Van Buren.*

PRESIDENT POLK

Builder: New York Shipbuilding Corporation, Camden, New Jersey.
Completed: March 1921.
Gross tonnage: 10513.
Dimensions: 522ft × 62ft. Depth 42ft.
Engines: Two four-cylinder, triple expansion.
Screws: Twin.
Watertight bulkheads: Thirteen.
Decks: Three.
Normal speed: 14 knots.
Passenger accommodation: 140 in a single class.
Maiden voyage: New York—Plymouth—Cherbourg —Bremen—Danzig on April 8, 1922, as *President Polk*.

Built for the United States Government and christened *Granite State*. Managed by the United States Mail Line until taken over by the United States Lines when the former went bankrupt in August 1921. Renamed *President Polk* in 1922. She and her four sisters are classified as cargo-passenger liners. Engaged in the London—New York service until sold to the Dollar Line in September 1923 with delivery in early 1924. Consolidated into the American President Lines in 1938 and renamed *President Taylor* in 1940. Stranded off Canton Island in the Pacific Ocean and abandoned on February 13, 1943.

Sister ships: *President Adams, President Garfield, President Monroe,* and *President Van Buren.*

PRESIDENT ROOSEVELT

Builder: New York Shipbuilding Corporation, Camden, New Jersey, USA.
Completed: January 1922.
Gross tonnage: 13869.
Dimensions: 535ft × 72ft. Depth 41ft.
Engines: Four steam turbines, single-reduction geared.
Screws: Twin.
Normal speed: 18 knots.
Passenger accommodation: 320 cabin and 324 third class.
Maiden voyage: New York–Plymouth–Cherbourg –Bremen on February 18, 1922, as *Peninsula State.*

Built for the United States Government and christened *Peninsula State.* Transferred to the United States Lines in 1922 and renamed *President Pierce* in May 1922; *President Roosevelt* in late 1922. Engaged in the New York–Cobh–London service mid-1932 when she was employed in the New York–Plymouth–Le Havre–Hamburg run with a call at Le Havre–Southampton–Cobh homeward. She is classified as a cargo-passenger liner. Requisitioned for troop work in 1941 and renamed *Joseph T. Dickman.* Sold for scrap in 1948.
Sister ship: *President Harding.*

PRESIDENT VAN BUREN

Builder: New York Shipbuilding Corporation,
  Camden, New Jersey, USA.
Completed: October 1920.
Gross tonnage: 10533.
Dimensions: 522ft × 62ft. Depth 42ft.
Engines: Two four-cylinder, triple expansion.
Screws: Twin.
Watertight bulkheads: Thirteen.
Decks: Three.
Normal speed: 14 knots.
Passenger accommodation: 140 in a single
  class.
Maiden voyage: New York—Boulogne—London on
  September 20, 1921.

Built for the United States Government and christened *Old North State*. Managed by the United
States Mail Line until taken over by the US Lines
on August 31, 1921 when the former went bankrupt. Renamed *President Van Buren* in 1922.
Employed in the New York—London service until
sold to the Dollar Line in September 1923 with

delivery in early 1924. Consolidated into the
American President Lines in 1938 and renamed
President Fillmore in 1940. Converted to a hospital
ship in 1942 and renamed *Marigold*. Sold for
scrap in 1948.
Sister ships: *President Adams, President Garfield, President Monroe,* and *President Polk.*

REPUBLIC

Builder: Harland & Wolff Ltd, Belfast, Ireland.
Completed: September 1907.
Gross tonnage: 17910.
Dimensions: 600ft × 68ft. Depth 52ft.
Engines: Two four-cylinder, quadruple expansion.
Screws: Twin.
Watertight bulkheads: Eleven.
Decks: Five.
Normal speed: 14 knots.
Passenger accommodation: 324 first, 125 second and 3000 third and steerage.
Maiden voyage: New York–Plymouth–Cherbourg–Bremen on April 29, 1924.

Built for Furness, Withy & Co and christened *Servian*. Sold to the Hamburg-America Line upon completion and renamed *President Grant*. Interned at New York in August 1914 and seized by the United States Government on April 4, 1917, and converted into a troopship. Transferred to the United States Lines in 1924 and ran under the name of *President Buchanan* for a time until renamed *Republic* in 1924. Employed in the New York–Channel ports–Bremen service. She was refitted for oil fuel in 1927 and converted to a cabin-class ship, her other class accommodations having been done away with. She was built with six masts and had her third and fourth removed at the time of her overhaul. Proceeded on her last commercial voyage for the United States Lines in June 1931 from Hamburg–Southampton–Cherbourg and home to New York. Returned back to the United States War Department in 1931 and laid up. Recalled once again for troop work at the outbreak of World War II. She was later utilised as a hospital ship in 1945 and decommissioned in February 1946. Laid up and sold for scrap at Baltimore, Maryland, in 1952.

UNITED STATES

Builder: Newport News Shipbuilding & Drydock Co, Newport News, Virginia, USA.
Completed: 1952.
Gross tonnage: 50924.
Dimensions: 990ft × 102ft. Depth 72ft.
Engines: Four steam turbines, double-reduction geared.
Screws: Quadruple.
Decks: Seven.
Normal speed: 33 knots.
Passenger accommodation: 882 first, 685 cabin and 718 tourist class.
Maiden voyage: New York–Le Havre–Southampton on July 3, 1952.
Last voyage: Bremerhaven–Southampton–Le Havre–New York on November 1, 1969.
Officers and crew: 1068.

Employed in the New York–Le Havre–Southampton service with a call at Cobh in the summer and on to Bremerhaven in winter. She is also used for cruising on occasion. Won the Blue Riband on her maiden voyage from the Cunard Line's *Queen Mary* by making the run from Ambrose Lighthouse to Bishop Rock in 3 days, 10 hours and 40 minutes at a speed of 35.59 knots. She is the largest merchant ship ever built in the United States of America at a cost of over $73 million dollars. The *United States* is the Lines' flagship and the recaptress of the Blue Riband lost for over a century by the United States of America. Equipped with motion stabilisers and fully air-conditioned, she is the fastest ship in the world with a potential speed of over 36 knots. She was designed with wartime specifications in mind having a troop capacity for 14,000 fully equipped men. Her superstructure is of aluminium and she is claimed to be virtually fireproof, with all her interior funiture constructed out of lightweight metals. Laid up on November 8, 1969, at Newport News as a result of the expiration of the Line's operating-differential-subsidy agreement with the Federal Government. Since the termination of this subsidy in 1969, losses for the fiscal year of 1970 were between four and five million dollars.

(See Notes on p. 223.)

WASHINGTON

Builder: New York Shipbuilding Corporation, Camden, New Jersey, USA.
Completed: 1933.
Gross tonnage: 23626.
Dimensions: 705ft × 86ft. Depth 47ft.
Engines: Six steam turbines, single-reduction geared.
Screws: Twin.
Watertight bulkheads: Eleven.
Decks: Six.
Normal speed: 20 knots.
Passenger accommodation: 500 cabin, 500 tourist and 106 third class.
Maiden voyage: New York–Cobh–Plymouth–Le Havre–Hamburg on May 10, 1933.

Engaged in the New York–Channel ports–Hamburg service and cruising. The *Washington* ran to Genoa for a time but ceased in July 1940 when hostilities began to worsen in Europe. She was then re-routed to cruising in American waters until United States entered the war, when she was requisitioned for troop work in 1941 and renamed *Mount Vernon*. This was the second transport to bear this name, the first having been an ex-German liner of World War I. Recovered her former name in 1945 and was chartered from the US Maritime Commission. She now carried her complement of passengers in a single class and ran to Cobh–Southampton–Le Havre–Hamburg and calling at Halifax homeward from February 1948 until October 12, 1951, when she made her last voyage for the United States Lines from Southampton to New York and was turned over to the United States Department of Commerce who utilised her to transport troops and their families between New York and Bremerhaven. Laid up in the Hudson River after her repatriation work and was sold to shipbreakers at Port Newark, New Jersey, in July 1965 in a rusted state that the years in reserve had brought about.
Sister ship: *Manhattan.*

GENERAL NOTES

CUNARD LINE

The *Adriatic, Albertic* and *Calgaric* were soon sold to shipbreakers by the end of 1934 and did not become liners in the service of the newly born Cunard-White Star Line.

The *Aurania* was to be a sister of the *Alaunia* and *Andania* but was completed as a transport and sunk by a torpedo fifteen miles from Inishtrahull, Ireland, on February 4, 1918, with the loss of eight lives.

The *Orduna* was chartered from the Royal Mail Packet Co for their Liverpool—New York service from November 1, 1914, until sometime in 1919 and was subsequently returned to them.

Note: Many Anchor liners such as the *Transylvania*, 1914, *Tuscania* 1915, and *Cameronia* 1910, were managed by the Cunard Line during World War I and were all lost in the course of the war. *Caledonia* 1925, *Transylvania* 1925, *Tuscania* 1922, and *California* 1923 were all chartered by the Cunard Line for a time between the mid-twenties until around 1930 and were painted in Cunard Line colours.

Adriatic	*(Launched)* 1906	*(Gross tons)*	24679
Albertic	1923		18940
Aurania	1916		13936
Calgaric	1918		16063
Orduna	1914		15507

FRENCH LINE

The *Savoie* was taken from the Jugoslavenski Lloyd in late 1939 while under the name of *Kraljica Marija*, formerly the *Araguaya* of the Royal Mail Lines. She was used for war services and sunk on November 8, 1942, never having sailed as a passenger ship for the French Line.

HOLLAND-AMERICA LINE

The *Pennland* was purchased from Arnold Bernstein in 1939 and was fitted out as a transport under the colours of the Holland-America Line. She was sunk by German aircraft on April 25, 1941, while *en route* from Alexandria, Egypt, to Athens, Greece, to evacuate British troops.
Sister ship: *Westernland*.

The *Statendam* was acquired by the British in 1917 and converted to a transport under the name of *Justicia* with the White Star Line acting as managers. On July 19, 1918, she was hit by two torpedoes from U-64 while *en route* to New York. She remained afloat after impact and had almost made it to Lock Swilly, Ireland, when the U-54 and U-124 dispatched her the following morning. There were no troops on board when this mishap occurred, but there was a loss of ten lives.

The *Zuiderdam* was to be a sister of the *Westerdam* had she not been sunk by the Germans in 1940 to block the New Waterway, Holland. She was raised in 1946, but found to be beyond repair was sold for scrap in Belgium two years later.

The *Westernland* was also purchased from Arnold Bernstein in 1939 and utilised as a transport by the British under the colours of the Holland-America Line. In January 1943 she was sold to the Admiralty for conversion to a destroyer depot ship, however, she remained as a transport until sold for scrap in July 1947.
Sister ship: *Pennland*.

Pennland	*(Launched)* 1922	*(Gross tons)*	16082
Statendam	1917		32324
Westernland	1918		16479
Zuiderdam	1946		12150

NORTH GERMAN LLOYD

The *Columbus* was ceded to Britain when completed as a World War I reparation and sold to the White Star Line by the British Shipping Controller in 1922 and renamed *Homeric*.

The *Kaiser Friedrich* was rejected by the North German Lloyd after nine trial voyages because she failed to meet the contract speed of her builders, F. Schichau.

The *Munchen* was also like the *Columbus* ceded to Britain in March 1923 when completed and sold to the Royal Mail Steam Packet Co and renamed *Ohio*.

Columbus	*(Launched)* 1920	*(Gross tons)*	34351
Kaiser Friedrich	1897		12480
Munchen	1923		18940

POLISH OCEAN LINES

The *Chrobry* was built for the Line in 1939 as a sister to the *Sobieski*, she was converted to a transport and destroyed at the battle of Narvik, Norway, on June 19, 1940 when she was bombed and set afire. There was some loss of life.
Sister ship: *Sobieski*.

Chrobry	*(Launched)* 1939	*(Gross tons)*	11,500

SWEDISH-AMERICAN LINES

Anticipating a heavy traffic of visitors for the Gothenburg Tercentenary Jubilee in 1923, the Line chartered the Holland-America Line's *Noordam* from March 1922 until December 1924.

The second *Stockholm* was launched in May 1938 and destroyed by fire at Trieste whilst fitting-out. The destroyed hulk was sold for scrapping.

The third *Stockholm* met with a similar fate after her construction in Trieste, Italy. Unable to reach Sweden by the Skagerrak blockade she was sold to the Italian Government and converted to a transport under the name of *Sabaudia*. Sunk by allied bombers at Trieste on July 6, 1944. Refloated and scrapped in 1949–50.

Kungsholm	*(Launched)* 1902	*(Gross tons)*	12531
Westernland	1918		16479
Zuiderdam	1946		12150

NOTES FOR THE REVISED 1979 EDITION
FEATURING FINAL DISPOSITIONS OF SHIPS

CUNARD LINE

II Carmania. Sold to the Russian States Lines in 1973. Presently in their service under the name *Leonid Sobinov.*

II Caronia. Sold for scrap in early 1974 in Taiwan for $3.5 million.

III Franconia. Sold to the Russian States Lines in 1973 for approximately £1,000,000. Renamed *Fedor Shalyapin* and presently in their service.

Queen ELizabeth 2. Last world-cruise from New York on January 10, 1975, with cabin prices ranging from $4,800 to $86,240 for the 80-day trip.

FRENCH LINE

II Antilles. Sold to American scrappers on March 12, 1971.

III France. Sold to Saudi Arabian entrepreneur Akram Ojjeh for conversion to a floating casino. This did not materialize, and the liner was sold in early July 1979 to Norwegian shipowner Knut Kloster. Renamed *Norway* and presently in his service.

III Lafayette. Broken up by June 1938.

GREEK LINE

Olympia. Settled into a cruise service out of Piraeus to Istanbul-Izmir-Haifa-Cyprus-Rhodes from April 5, 1974, to November, when she was laid up pending sale.

Queen Anna Maria. Sold to Carnival Cruises for $3.2 million in 1975 and renamed *Carnival.* Presently in their service.

HOLLAND-AMERICA LINE

II Noordam. Sold to Cantieri Navali del Golfo at La Spezia, Italy, for scrap. Arrived for breaking up on February 14, 1967.

IV Rotterdam. Sold for scrap in December 1939 to Frank Rijsdiyk at Hendrik Ido Ambacht and broken up by March 1940.

Westerdam. Broken up by March 1965.

ITALIAN LINES

Cristoforo Colombo. Sold to the Venezuelan government for approximately $6.8 million in 1977. Now used as a hotel ship for employees of a steelworks near Mantanzas on the Orinoco River.

Donizetti. Withdrawn from service on October 15, 1976. Sold in June 1977 to Cantieri Navali del Golfo at La Spezia, Italy, for scrapping for 300,000,000 lire.

Leonardo da Vinci. Sold to the Costa Line in October 1976. Presently in their service.

Michelangelo. Sold to the Iranian government in late 1976 for approximately $9 million for use as a home and training ground for Iranian Navy officers and their families.

Orazio. Broken up by March 1940.

Raffaello. Sold to the Iranian government in late 1976 for $9 million for use as a home for naval officers and their families.

Vulcania. Scrapped in Taiwan in early 1974.

NORTH GERMAN LLOYD LINE

V Bremen. Sold to Chandris Lines in January 1972 for $3 million. Renamed *Regina Magna* and is presently in their service.

Potsdam. Sold for scrap in Karachi, Pakistan, in May 1976 and broken up by October of that year.

POLISH OCEAN LINES

Batory. Sold for scrap to Yau Wing Co., Ltd., Hong Kong. Left Gdynia on March 30, 1971, arriving for demolition on May 11. Dismantling operations began on June 1, 1971.

PORTUGUESE LINE

Imperio. Sold for scrap in Kaohsiung, Taiwan, and arrived there on March 24, 1974. Demolition commenced on August 2 and was completed by September.

Infante Dom Henrique. Converted to a workers hotel in 1978 in Portugal after her sale to the Companhia Portuguesa de Transportes Maritimes in 1974.

Patria. Withdrawn from service on May 20, 1973, and sold to shipbreakers in Taipei in July.

Santa Maria. Sold to Galbraith-Wrightsen for breaking up in Kaohsiung, Taiwan, by the Yuita Steel & Iron Works Co., Ltd. Arrived on July 19, 1973, with work commencing in September.

Vera Cruz. Sold to Galbraith-Wrightsen. Arrived in Kaohsiung, Taiwan, on April 19, 1973, for breaking up by the Yuita Steel & Iron Works Co., Ltd.

SPANISH LINE

Begona. Sold for scrap to Desguaces Varela in Castellon, Spain, arriving at the shipbreakers yard on November 28, 1974.

II Covadonga. Arrived at Castellon, Spain, on April 4, 1973, for demolition by Messrs. Desguaces Varela Davalillo.

Guadalupe. Sold for scrap to Desguaces Varela. Arrived at the shipbreakers yard in Castellon, Spain, on April 12, 1973.

SWEDISH-AMERICAN LINE

II Gripsholm. Sold to the Michael Karageorgis Line and taken over by them on November 26, 1975, at Sandefjord, Norway. Renamed *Navarino* and is presently in their service.

IV Kungsholm. Arrived at Newcastle-on-Tyne, Great Britain, on September 18, 1975, and was taken over by her new owners, Flagship Cruises. Presently in their service.

UNITED STATES LINES

II America. Sold to Venture Cruise Lines in early 1978 for $2.5 million and renamed *Americabut.* After a few unsuccessful voyages out of New York, the line went bankrupt.

United States. Sold to Richard Hadley, a Seattle, Washington, property-developer, in September 1978 for $5 million for his newly formed United States Cruises, based in Los Angeles. Presently in their service.

ALPHABETICAL LIST OF SHIPS